30-SECOND
ANTHROPOLOGY

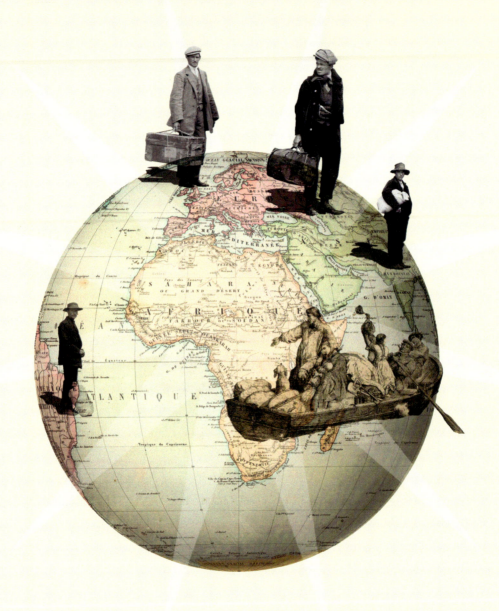

30-SECOND
ANTHROPOLOGY

The 50 most important ideas
in the study of being human,
each explained in half a minute

Editor
Simon Underdown

Contributors
Russell Adams
Sue Black
Brad K. Blitz
Jason Danely
Ken Dark
Jan Freedman
Charlotte Houldcroft
Marta Mirazón Lahr
Michael Bang Petersen
Joshua Pollard
David Shankland
Djuke Veldhuis

Illustrations
Nicky Ackland-Snow

IVY PRESS

First published in the UK in 2018 by
Ivy Press
An imprint of The Quarto Group
The Old Brewery, 6 Blundell Street
London N7 9BH,United Kingdom
T (0)20 7700 6700 **F** (0)20 7700 8066
www.QuartoKnows.com

British Library Cataloguing-in-
Publication Data
A catalogue record for this
book is available from the
British Library.

ISBN: 978-1-78240-545-0

This book was conceived,
designed and produced by
Ivy Press
58 West Street, Brighton BN1 2RA, UK

Publisher **Susan Kelly**
Creative Director **Michael Whitehead**
Editorial Director **Tom Kitch**
Commissioning Editor **Stephanie Evans**
Project Editor **Joanna Bentley**
Designer **Ginny Zeal**
Picture researcher **Katie Greenwood**

Printed in China

10 9 8 7 6 5 4 3 2 1

CONTENTS

INTRODUCTION
Simon Underdown

Anthropology is the study of the most complex and contradictory species on the planet – us. Humans are not easy to understand and are even more difficult to explain. On paper, we are a relatively large naked form of ape with a big brain and an odd way of walking on two legs. Yet we have taken our ability to use culture, such as tools, to solve biological problems and conquered the world. Around 2 million years ago our ancestors started to look and behave in a recognizably human way. From then on our ability to shape the environment intensified to the level we find ourselves at today.

We share 98 per cent of our DNA with chimpanzees but our genetic similarity is offset by the gulf in intelligence and culture between us and our evolutionary cousins.

This book is an instruction manual for human beings. It will help you understand how we evolved from a chimp-like ancestor to being able to send rockets to Mars. Humans are unquestionably special and occupy a unique place in the history of the planet. Our brains are the most complex thing in the known universe and nothing approaches the intricacy and sophistication of human thought. But when we compare our behaviour to that of other primates the gulf is perhaps not as great as we might like to think. Chimps and many other species of primate use tools and display highly advanced levels of intelligence. Yet the gap in ability and achievement remains insurmountable. Humans today can be found on every continent and, alongside our technology, we have developed a bewilderingly large range of religions, beliefs and cultural practices. No other species comes close to being as odd as us. This is what anthropology tries to explain and it is perhaps one of the most difficult questions in science.

What's in a name?

Anthropology is broadly split into two subdisciplines: social anthropology and biological anthropology. Social anthropology explores societies and cultures in all their diversity and is a largely self-sufficient subject that draws on its own methods. Biological anthropology blurs the lines between traditional academic subjects, and it uses methods from areas as diverse as genetics, physics and archaeology to explain human beings within the context of evolution – especially how our biology interacts with our culture. Traditionally, anthropology is not a subject with good PR and outside of universities it is not well known or well understood. Anthropology still conjures up images of men in pith helmets somewhere 'exotic'. But despite this misapprehension anthropology is 'done' by a wide range of people, both at home and abroad, who may not use the label but are still 'doing' anthropology. Historically, the fifth-century BCE Greek historian Herodotus was perhaps the first anthropologist and his, albeit sometimes fictional, accounts of foreign cultures and behaviours has a distinctly anthropological theme. The roots of the subject as an academic discipline belong to the nineteenth century, when ethnographers began to study people in the expanding European empires – often as means of reinforcing ideas of European supremacy. In the twentieth and twenty-first centuries, a backlash against such outmoded thinking has created a context in which today human variation is championed and our shared evolutionary heritage is celebrated.

Herodotus wrote about the known world in a distinctly anthropological way: identifying variation and reflecting on shared traits.

How this book works

This book presents 50 of the most important ideas and concepts in twenty-first-century anthropology. Each section has three parts: the 30-Second Anthropology describes a key

Each generation of humans has developed increasingly sophisticated technology to assist in every aspect of life - with cutting edge ideas quickly being surpassed by those of future generations.

anthropological concept in detail, the 3-Minute Descent places the idea in the wider context of being human and the 3-Second Origin provides the essence of the idea in a single sentence.

The book is divided into seven chapters that provide an overview of how we have become human and what being human means. **Evolution** explores the evolutionary history of humans and creates a context for understanding the roots of modern human biology, culture and diversity. **The Human Species** demolishes the idea of different human races before explaining how we understand patterns of variation and diversity in the modern world. **Materials** examines how we use culture and technology to help shape the world around us and manipulate the environment. **Socialization & Communication** considers the complex ways in which humans organize themselves into groups and how we interact with each other using verbal and nonverbal means of communication. Humans are one of the most widely distributed species on the planet and in **Migration** we are concerned with how humans have moved around the world in the past and how modern movement contributes to our thoughts about identity and belonging. **Ideas** are the foundation upon which humans have shaped the planet and guided our cultural evolution and this chapter examines key lines of thinking and how they have shaped who we are. The book concludes with **Modern Peoples**, which contemplates the future of our species and how we deal with the challenges created by our shared evolutionary journey into the twenty-first century.

Overall the aim of the book is not to provide an exhaustive list of everything anthropology is and everything anthropologists do – honestly, that would be a very dull read. Instead we have offered you a reflection of what has influenced our evolution and development as humans and how we can try to understand our place in a dynamic and unstable world.

EVOLUTION OF HOMININS

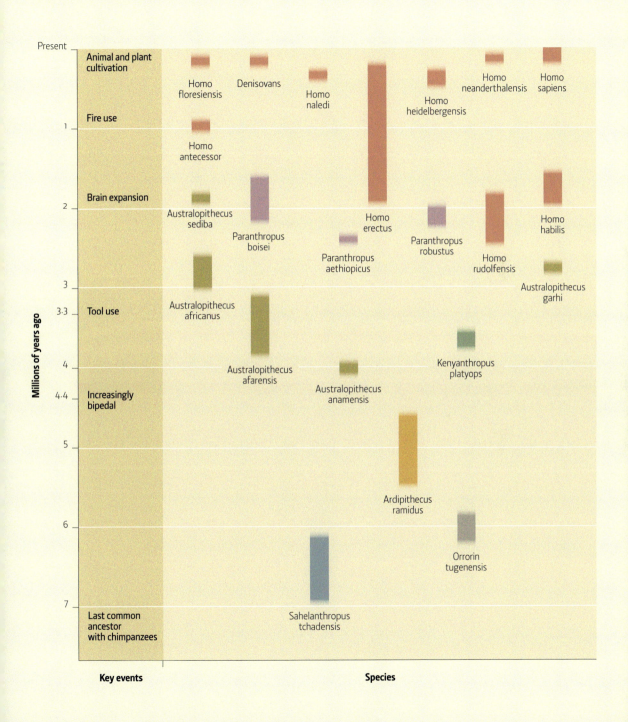

Millions of years ago

Present —

Key events (left column):
- Animal and plant cultivation
- Fire use
- Brain expansion
- Tool use
- Increasingly bipedal
- Last common ancestor with chimpanzees

Time axis: 1, 2, 3, 3·3, 4, 4·4, 5, 6, 7

Species:
- Homo floresiensis
- Denisovans
- Homo naledi
- Homo heidelbergensis
- Homo neanderthalensis
- Homo sapiens
- Homo antecessor
- Australopithecus sediba
- Paranthropus boisei
- Homo erectus
- Paranthropus robustus
- Homo habilis
- Paranthropus aethiopicus
- Homo rudolfensis
- Australopithecus garhi
- Australopithecus africanus
- Australopithecus afarensis
- Kenyanthropus platyops
- Australopithecus anamensis
- Ardipithecus ramidus
- Orrorin tugenensis
- Sahelanthropus tchadensis

Key events   **Species**

EVOLUTION

Acheulean handaxe A type of stone tool technology that first appeared around 1.8 million years ago in Africa and was typified by being 'worked' on both sides and by its teardrop shape.

apex predator An organism that sits at the top of a food chain or web that nothing else preys on. Humans became apex predators around 2 million years ago.

Australopithecines A genus of hominin that evolved in East Africa around 4 million years ago, spreading as far as South Africa, before becoming extinct around 2 million years ago. Six species are currently known but their exact relationship to the genus *Homo* remains a source of great debate in anthropology.

Broca's Area Named after the French anatomist Paul Broca, who first associated it with language, Broca's Area is part of the frontal lobe of the hominin brain. It is generally found in the dominant hemisphere of the brain and is linked to aspects of speech production.

Denisovan hominin Name given to a species of the genus *Homo* from the Altai mountains in Siberia. Only tiny fragments of fossils have been found and the species is known almost entirely from ancient DNA, which shows that the Denisovans interbred with both us and the Neanderthals.

DNA Deoxyribonucleic acid is a chain-like structure found in the chromosomes of almost every living thing apart from a handful of viruses. As the primary genetic material of an organism it controls the production of proteins and transmits inherited traits, acting as the blueprint for development.

DNA chain DNA is arranged in a double-helix chain-like structure. The model was first proposed by James Watson and Francis Crick in 1953. Chains of DNA – called polynucleotides – are held together by hydrogen bonds.

genome All the genetic material of an individual organism.

genus (pl genera) The name given to a group of closely related species. Genera, along with the species, are part of the binomial naming system developed by Linnaeus.

great apes Also known as the hominids, they are a family in the Linnaean classification system that includes humans, chimps, bonobos, gorillas and orangutans.

Homo erectus The first 'human' hominin appeared around 2 million years ago in East Africa before rapidly expanding its range to Asia and Europe.

Homo sapiens Our own species name, which means 'wise man'. All living humans today can trace our ancestry back to East Africa around 200,000 years ago.

Hoxne hand axe Found at Hoxne in Suffolk and described by the British antiquarian John Frere in 1797, this has been dated to around 400,000 years ago.

Linnaean classification Developed by the Swedish botanist Carl Linnaeus and published in 1735, this is still the basis of taxonomy – the rules by which organisms are grouped by kingdom, phylum, class, order, family, genus and species.

Lomekwian The earliest known form of stone tool type, found at Lomekwi in Kenya and dated to 3.3 million years ago.

'Mitochondrial Eve' The most recent female common ancestor of all living humans. Mitochondrial DNA is inherited only from mothers and 'Eve' is the base of that line. It does not mean that Eve was the only woman, rather that she is the only surviving maternal line, as over time the mitochondrial DNA of women not having children or whose children did not have offspring dies out.

Mousterian tools The form of stone tool most closely associated with Neanderthals. Found especially in Europe between approximately 160,000–40,000 years ago.

Omo 1 The name of the earliest known *Homo sapiens* fossil. It was found in the Omo Valley, Ethiopia in 1967.

palaeoanthropology The branch of anthropology that explores human fossils.

phenotype (phenotypically) / genotype (genotypically) The phenotype is the outward appearance of an organism and is the result of the genotype (the part of an organism's genome that controls how it develops) interacting with the environment.

Primate order A level of the Linnaean taxonomic system that includes all hominins (living and extinct), apes, monkeys, tarsiers, lemurs and lorises.

Sahelanthropus tchadensis The earliest known hominin, excavated in Chad in 2001–2 and dated to 7 million years ago.

THE HOMININS

the 30-second anthropology

Hominins are our distant

ancestors. More precisely, they are a subfamily of the Linnaean classification of the Primate order that includes humans and all our evolutionary ancestors. There are currently seven known genera (the groups that contain species) and 15–30 species – the uncertainty arises because classification of species depends on whether variations in anatomy are interpreted as internal to the species or external, making a separate species. Although ancient DNA can help this problem with more recent evolution, if we go back more than a few hundred thousand years we are forced to rely on the lumps and bumps in a small number of fragmentary fossils. Hominin evolution is a 7-million-year history and for the first 5 million years our ancestors – from *Sahelanthropus tchadensis* (7 million years ago) to the *Australopithecines* (5 million years ago onwards) – would have looked very apelike to our eyes; it is perhaps easiest to picture an odd-looking chimpanzee. There was nothing remotely human about them. It is best to think of the period from 7–5 million years ago as 'hominin evolution'. It is not until 2 million years ago that we see the start of human-like hominins that, although different from us, shared some of our abilities, behaviours and genes.

3-SECOND ORIGIN
Of the seven known genera of hominin, one survives – the genus homo; of the eight to ten species belonging to this genus, one survives – *Homo sapiens*.

3-MINUTE DESCENT
Hominins used to be called hominids and were thought to be distinct from the other African great apes. In order to better describe the close evolutionary relationship between the great apes, a new subfamily level was created. The family group 'hominid' now contains all the great apes, not just the species of the human lineage; and the newly created subfamily name 'hominin' (with associated subfamilies for chimps and gorillas) contains all the species of the human evolutionary lineage.

RELATED TOPICS
See also
THE NEANDERTHALS
page 22

HOMO SAPIENS
page 24

ANCIENT DNA
page 28

3-SECOND BIOGRAPHIES
EUGÈNE DUBOIS
1858–1940
Dutch palaeoanthropologist and geologist, who excavated fossils he called *Pithecanthropus erectus*, now *Homo erectus*

RAYMOND DART
1893–1988
Australian anthropologist whose pioneering work in South Africa included the analysis and naming of the first fossil of *Australopithecus africanus*

30-SECOND TEXT
Simon Underdown

We are the only surviving hominin species yet, as recently as 250,000 years ago, there were at least five hominin species spread across the world.

BRAIN DEVELOPMENT

the 30-second anthropology

The human brain is perhaps the most remarkable thing to have ever evolved. Our brains allow us to communicate via symbolic text, externalize concepts and share complex ideas across generations. While all primates share a general brain pattern, the human brain is remarkable for its size (far larger than would be expected for a primate of our size) and how we have used it to shape our cultural evolution. The first hominins had small brains, around 450 cm^3 (27 in^3), which is comparable to those of chimps. Around 2 million years ago our ancestors' brains started to increase in size almost exponentially. Beginning with *Homo erectus*, this pattern continued until we reach the modern human brain size of c. 1250 cm^3 (76 in^3). The exact cause of this increase is a matter of speculation but it seems likely that extra meat entered the diet via stone tool use, fuelling the bigger brains needed to manage relationships in large social groups. The benefits of this process include complex language and the ability to develop ever more sophisticated cultural solutions to biological problems. Our brains today are no different to those of the first *Homo sapiens* – the only difference is the technology we have developed through each generation building on the achievements of its predecessor.

3-SECOND ORIGIN
The human brain is capable of immensely complex processes and needs 20 per cent of our daily calorie intake to tick over – more than any other organ.

3-MINUTE DESCENT
Primate brains usually double in size between birth and adulthood but human brains triple in size. This allows our brain to reach its full size but still pass through the birth canal, which is unusually narrow because it is adapted for walking on two legs. This period of postnatal brain growth, known as the fourth trimester, is thought to allow our minds to develop extra neuron links, which are associated with our advanced intelligence.

RELATED TOPICS
See also
TOOLS
page 18

THE NEANDERTHALS
page 22

HOMO SAPIENS
page 24

3-SECOND BIOGRAPHIES
GALEN OF PERGAMON
129–c. 200/c. 216 CE
Greek physician whose experiments were the first to demonstrate that the brain controls muscles via the nervous system

PAUL BROCA
1824–80
French physician and anthropologist who led pioneering work on the area of the brain responsible for speech production – now called Broca's Area

30-SECOND TEXT
Simon Underdown

The human brain is almost three times larger than the chimp's, enabling our complex thought processes.

TOOLS

the 30-second anthropology

Humans, while not the only

tool-using species, are the only living species that is totally reliant on tools for its survival. The earliest known stone tools date to 3.3 million years ago – although it is highly likely that tools made from wood or bone were being used before this, but have not survived. The earliest tools were large stones that had flakes removed to leave a heavy hammer to crush bone. The flakes could be used as cutting edges for slicing meat or plant material. Over time, stone tools became much more sophisticated. From 1.8 million years ago the teardrop-shaped Acheulean handaxe was the dominant technology and accompanied hominin species out of Africa. The Neanderthals made tools known as 'Mousterian', based on a general pattern that could be worked to produce a wide range of shapes for cutting, hafting onto spears and piercing leather. In contrast, early *Homo sapiens* used a flaking technique to produce multiple tools for different tasks. Today we use tools in almost every aspect of our lives. The use of tools in the past allowed us to expand and cope with new environments. In doing so we tipped the balance so that we can no longer survive without them.

RELATED TOPICS
See also
THE HOMININS
page 14

THE NEANDERTHALS
page 22

HOMO SAPIENS
page 24

3-SECOND ORIGIN
The earliest known stone tools were made by an unknown hominin species about 3.3 million years ago at Lomekwi in modern-day Kenya.

3-MINUTE DESCENT
Tool use is not a purely human behaviour and is known in many primate species, as well as other mammals and birds. What makes human tool use different is how we have used tools to shape the environment to suit our needs. The first stone tool from 3.3 million years ago was used to crush bone to extract the highly nutritious marrow. This was the technological ancestor of using aeroplanes to transport food across the globe today.

3-SECOND BIOGRAPHIES
JOHN FRERE
1740–1807
English antiquarian who was one of the first to argue that stone tools belonged to the 'Old Stone Age'. He carried out pioneering work at Hoxne, Suffolk, England

SIR JOSEPH PRESTWICH
1812–96
English geologist whose work on the Tertiary Period was instrumental in demonstrating the age of stone tools found in gravel beds at Saint-Acheul, France

30-SECOND TEXT
Simon Underdown

From stone axes to aeroplanes, tools have been central to human development.

FIRE

the 30-second anthropology

Humans and fire have a very

special relationship. Almost all human cultures have a tradition of a central fire around which groups congregate. In modern Western culture the role of the kitchen as a central point in homes is derived from that of the first campfires hundreds of thousands of years ago. Early fire use is notoriously difficult to identify in the archaeological record because it is not always possible to differentiate between naturally occurring and human-controlled fire. The first definite evidence of fire use dates to 1 million years ago, but there are claims that fire was used as long as 1.4 million years ago. The first hominin to intentionally manipulate fire was *Homo erectus* – a species that can lay claim to being the first 'human'. Our use of fire is a perfect example of how humans use culture to solve biological problems. Fire allows us to cook, which broadens the range of food we can eat. It acts as a source of light and protection against predators, and its position as a focal point for group activity strengthened group bonds and stimulated social development. From a practical point of view the light provided by fire would have extended the time our ancestors could spend on tool production, enhancing our position as apex predators as we expanded into new environments.

RELATED TOPICS
See also
THE HOMININS
page 14

THE NEANDERTHALS
page 22

HOMO SAPIENS
page 24

3-SECOND ORIGIN
As a source of heat and light and a focal point for social activity, fire has been central to human development.

3-MINUTE DESCENT
Our ancestors' use of fire broadened their diet by allowing inedible foods, such as starchy and fibrous roots, to be cooked. Cooking food can massively increase the calories released during digestion and kill harmful parasites and bacteria found in meat. Fire also provided a central focus for our ancestors. Neanderthal cave sites have been excavated that have central hearths around which a variety of activities took place, as we can see in the archaeological record.

3-SECOND BIOGRAPHIES
HOMO ERECTUS
2 million years ago
The first hominin to use and control fire; evidence from Wonderwerk cave in South Africa shows controlled fire use 1 million years ago

HOMO HEIDELBERGENSIS
500,000 years ago
The last common ancestor of *Homo sapiens* and the Neanderthals lived in Europe and Africa around 500,000 years ago and used fire to harden wooden spear tips

30-SECOND TEXT
Simon Underdown

Providing warmth, light, a way to cook and protection, fire allowed humans to shape the world to their needs.

THE NEANDERTHALS

the 30-second anthropology

The Neanderthals occupy a strange place in human evolution. First described in 1859, they were regarded for decades as quintessentially slow-witted, lumbering cavemen. The knuckle-dragging brute of popular image was the result of a nineteenth-century misdiagnosis of a fossil that got stuck in the popular imagination. More recently they have undergone an archaeological and genetic renaissance. Ancient DNA shows that they interbred with *Homo sapiens* several times and also with the little-known Denisovan hominins from the Altai mountains in Siberia. It also tells us about the genes we share and how we differ. We now have a much clearer image of the Neanderthals as Eurasia-dwelling humans who lived in groups of about 30–40, wore clothes, used fire, cared for their sick and produced coloured pigment for decoration. Neanderthals' brains were around 10 per cent bigger than ours; they had a slightly different body shape from *Homo sapiens* with a more protruding face, but detailed facial reconstructions nevertheless reveal a very 'human' face. The way they made tools, hunted and manipulated their environment suggests a highly sophisticated human species who would have used complex speech and perhaps shared many of the thought patterns and emotions we have.

RELATED TOPICS
See also
THE HOMININS
page 14

HOMO SAPIENS
page 24

ANCIENT DNA
page 28

3-SECOND ORIGIN
Everyone outside of Africa has 1–4 per cent Neanderthal DNA from interbreeding; so although they are phenotypically extinct, they genotypically still exist in many of us.

3-MINUTE DESCENT
Many of the behaviours we think of as especially 'human' are found in the Neanderthals – often before we started doing them. Archaeological evidence suggests that the Neanderthals buried their dead, made jewellery and built structures deep inside caves. Ancient DNA shows that we interbred with the Neanderthals and exchanged useful genes, especially those associated with disease resistance. The gap between us is almost invisible and we should see them as another fully human species.

3-SECOND BIOGRAPHIES
JOHANN KARL FUHLROTT
1803–77
German naturalist who recognized that bones found in the Neander Valley in Germany in 1856 belonged to a unique human species

MARCELLIN BOULE
1861–1942
French archaeologist who published the first description of a complete Neanderthal in 1920: *Les hommes fossiles – Éléments de paléontologie humaine*

30-SECOND TEXT
Simon Underdown

No longer the stupid brutes of popular imagination, the Neanderthals are now known to have been a sophisticated species.

HOMO SAPIENS

the 30-second anthropology

Homo sapiens is one of the most successful animal species to have ever existed. Humans are the last remaining hominin species and the only member of the genus homo to have colonized the entire planet. Based on fossil and genetic evidence, we can trace our direct ancestry back to East Africa around 200,000 years ago. We began to move beyond our African homeland some time after 100,000 years ago and interbred several times with Neanderthals in Asia and Europe, and the Denisovans in Siberia. Much has been made of our superiority to our Neanderthal cousins but our survival, and their extinction, has more to do with happenstance than innate superiority. Underlying our remarkable success is our extremely large brain. We are born before our brains have finished developing and the period of postnatal brain growth seems to be directly related to our ability to construct external cognitive processes: first language, then writing and now the internet. Humans don't need to remember useful information – we can externally store, share and retrieve it. Just as stone tools allowed us to move beyond our biological adaptations, so we can use an external brain to build on our success.

RELATED TOPICS
See also
THE HOMININS
page 14

THE NEANDERTHALS
page 22

ANCIENT DNA
page 28

3-SECOND ORIGIN
All living humans can trace their direct ancestry back to a small group of humans living in East Africa approximately 200,000 years ago.

3-MINUTE DESCENT
Assuming an average human generation span as 30 years, just over 6,666 generations separate humans living today from the earliest members of our species. A line containing one person from each generation holding hands would barely cover 11 km (7 miles): the distance from Hyde Park to the Millennium Dome in London or from the northern corner of Central Park to the WTC memorial in New York.

3-SECOND BIOGRAPHIES
OMO 1
195,000 years ago
Earliest known fossil to be given the label *Homo sapiens*, excavated 1967–74 by a team led by Richard Leakey at the site of Omo Kibish in Ethiopia

ÖTZI THE ICEMAN
died c. 3239–3105 BCE
Natural mummy, found preserved in the ice of the Ötztal Alps between the border of Austria and Switzerland in 1991; analysis suggests that he died from exposure

30-SECOND TEXT
Simon Underdown

Across the generations, the genes of **Homo sapiens** *have survived from origins around* **200,000 years ago.**

19 December 1944
Born in Nairobi, Kenya, the second of Louis and Mary Leakey's three sons

1968
Appointed director of the National Museums of Kenya

1968
Leads expedition to Koobi Fora, finding numbers of hominid fossils

1989
Appointed head of Kenya Wildlife Services. Stages a dramatic burning of confiscated elephant tusks

1993
Loses both legs below the knee in a plane crash

1997
Elected to Kenyan parliament representing the Safina party

1999
Appointed head of Kenya's Civil Service

2002
Joins the Department of Anthropology at Stony Brook University, New York

2015
Becomes chair of Kenya Wildlife Services

RICHARD LEAKEY

Palaeoanthropologist Richard

Leakey and his colleague and wife, Meave Leakey, have been the discoverers of several key fossils that mark major steps in the evolution of *Homo sapiens*. These include fossils relevant to the evolution of the apes from which humans derive, the emergence of the first true hominins who walked on two legs, the arrival of the first human-like creatures with bodies like us, the coming of more complex technology and a larger brain, and the first modern humans.

The son of Louis and Mary Leakey, pioneer anthropologists and archaeologists of Africa, the young Richard Leakey is a controversial role model for students. Abandoning formal education at the age of 16, he pursued various careers in East Africa – naturalist, safari guide, hunter and trapper – until he was drawn into the family business of palaeoanthropology: the search for the traces of early humans and their evolutionary history. Once set on this path, he shone: he had a great ability to find new sites, make significant discoveries and bring together and lead notable scientific teams – and in the process inspired many in and beyond the field of human evolution.

After working briefly on the Omo river in southern Ethiopia in the late 1960s, where he found what are still the earliest known fossils of our species, *Homo sapiens*, he went on to lead a project exploring first the eastern and then the western side of Lake Turkana in northern Kenya. His discoveries there completely changed our understanding of how humans evolved.

Richard Leakey has combined being at the forefront of palaeoanthropology with making major contributions to other aspects of life. From 1989–94 he was director of the Kenya Wildlife Service and spearheaded a campaign that drastically cut poaching. He founded a political party that helped open up multi-party democracy in Kenya, was head of the Kenyan civil service for three years and has since been a leading campaigner against corruption. Most recently he returned to palaeoanthropology and founded the Turkana Basin Institute, a Kenya-based research foundation to support and continue the research he has inspired, and in 2015 to the problem of wildlife conservation as Chair of Kenya Wildlife Services. He is a professor at Stony Brook University and a Fellow of the Royal Society, and one of the most extraordinary individuals of our times.

Marta Mirazón Lahr

ANCIENT DNA

the 30-second anthropology

Ancient DNA (aDNA) analysis is one of the most important developments within anthropology since Charles Darwin published *On the Origin of Species* in 1859. It allows the genetic code of people who lived many thousands of years ago to be analyzed, revealing data about their lives that is well beyond what traditional archaeology alone can provide. However, there are many problems facing the recovery, extraction and analysis of aDNA. Unlike modern genetic sampling (from saliva, hair, blood or semen, for example) ancient genetic samples are typically of very low quality – and they are much shorter than modern samples. This is because after death the DNA chain starts to degrade – a process directly related to time and temperature. The colder the location and the more recent the date the better the chances of recovering high-quality aDNA samples. The current oldest human sample, from a cave in northern Spain, is 400,000 years old but most aDNA samples are much younger. aDNA can be used to reconstruct how species have evolved, moved across time and space and, in the case of humans and Neanderthals, interbred and exchanged genes and diseases – all of which was unknown before aDNA.

3-SECOND ORIGIN
When ancient DNA was first recovered in 1984 from a museum specimen of a quagga it showed that DNA could survive well beyond death.

3-MINUTE DESCENT
Ancient DNA is a general term that refers to DNA recovered from any old biological material. While generally associated with archaeological bones and teeth, it can also be extracted from mummified tissues, cave earth sediments, ice cores and many other sources such as medical collections.

RELATED TOPICS
See also
THE NEANDERTHALS
page 22

HOMO SAPIENS
page 24

3-SECOND BIOGRAPHIES
ALLAN WILSON
1934–91
New Zealand-born biochemist, who with his PhD students Rebecca Cann and Mark Stoneking identified 'Mitochondrial Eve' – the African female common ancestor of all living humans

SVANTE PÄÄBO
1955–
Swedish geneticist whose team produced the first Neanderthal genome and discovered the Denisovan hominin based purely on ancient DNA

30-SECOND TEXT
Simon Underdown

Ancient DNA provides a unique window on to the past that cannot be opened with archaeology alone.

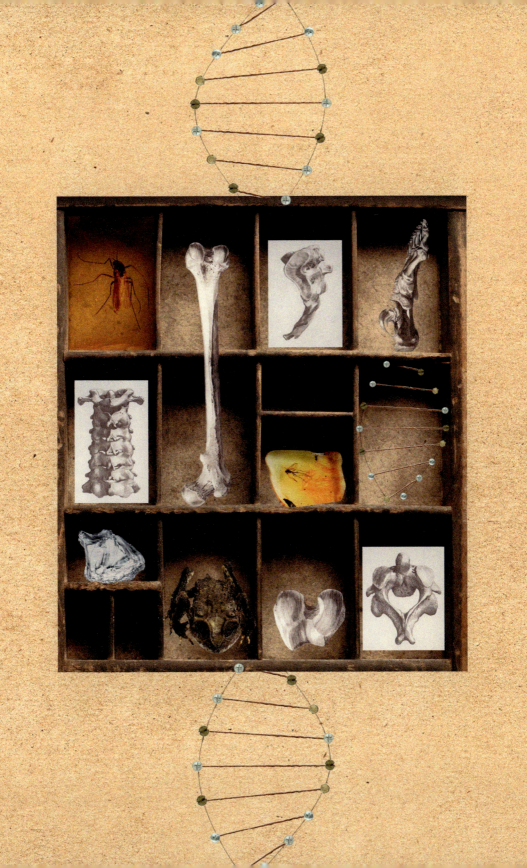

THE HUMAN SPECIES

THE HUMAN SPECIES
GLOSSARY

Aztecs A cultural group found in Central Mexico between the fourteenth and sixteenth centuries. Known mostly from archaeological evidence and the often lurid accounts written by Spanish colonialists.

Clovis culture An American Palaeo-Indian group that lived between 11,500–11,000 years ago, named after their distinctive stone tools first found at Clovis, New Mexico in the 1920s.

cultural relativism A theory in social anthropology developed by Franz Boas that argues that beliefs can only be understood in the context they come from.

DNA Deoxyribonucleic acid is a chain-like structure found in the chromosomes of almost every living thing apart from a handful of viruses. As the primary genetic material of an organism it controls the production of proteins and transmits inherited traits, acting as the blueprint for development.

ethnography The systematic social-cultural study of people, often referring to the written account of such research.

feminism An umbrella term for a broad range of thinking and movements that campaign for equal rights and opportunities for women.

hominin A Linnaean subfamily that includes humans and all of their ancestors after the split from the last common ancestor with chimps around 7 million years ago.

Homo erectus The first 'human' hominin appeared around 2 million years ago in East Africa before rapidly expanding its range to Asia and Europe.

Homo sapiens Our own species name, which means 'wise man'. All living humans today can trace our ancestry back to East Africa around 200,000 years ago.

humanism The idea that humans should use reason to improve the lives of all. It is often associated with atheism and has a strong science-based focus.

Inca The largest empire in the pre-Columbian Americas, its origins can be traced to the thirteenth century. The Incas were conquered by the Spanish in 1572.

indigenous people A term used to describe the earliest inhabitants of a region and their living descendants.

Inuit The groups of people who inhabit the Arctic areas of Alaska, Canada and Greenland. Modern Inuit are the indigenous ancestors of the original inhabitants who colonized the area around 5,000 years ago.

***kapa haka* dance** *Kapa haka* is a collection of Maori dance forms that are used to express tradition (well known from its use by the New Zealand rugby team).

Maya The Mayan civilization refers to several distinct cultures between 2000 BCE and 1697 (the date of the final Spanish conquest). Most well known is the Classic Period between 250–900 CE that saw the creation of complex city states and the famous Mayan calendar.

melanin A group of molecules produced in the skin that is responsible for variations in skin colour. In humans it evolved as a protection against UV radiation some time after 2 million years ago.

Neanderthal An advanced species of hominin that lived in Europe and Asia between about 250,000 and 30,000 years ago. They developed many advanced behaviours and interbred with humans several times. The reason behind their extinction remains one of the most intriguing questions in human evolution.

Out of Africa hypothesis The theory that argues *Homo sapiens* evolved from a recent common ancestor in Africa around 200,000 years ago before gradually spreading across the world some time after 100,000 years ago, replacing all of the other hominin species found in Europe and Asia such as the Neanderthals, Denisovans and *Homo floresiensis* (also known as the Hobbit). Analysis of ancient DNA shows that limited interbreeding took place, leaving echoes of the earlier inhabitants of Asia and Europe in all non-African people today.

palaeoanthropology The branch of anthropology that explores human fossils.

vitamin D Produced by the action of UV radiation on the skin, this vitamin ensures proper uptake of nutrients such as calcium by the intestines.

RACE

the 30-second anthropology

The idea of categorizing humans into groups is an old one: our immediate family, extended family, village, tribe, religion, region, nation – and a huge number of other social categories, including race. This reflects the rich cultural diversity that we as humans have created. But race has a specific biological meaning and is identical to the term 'subspecies', used for groups of organisms within a species that are genetically distinct from one another. In fact, we show a relatively low level of genetic diversity when compared to chimps and gorillas (a result of a population crash around 70,000 years ago when our total population size decreased to around 10,000 individuals). This means that there is next to no variation between a person from Africa, Europe or Asia – pick any two people at random from anywhere on the planet and they will be very closely related when you look at their DNA, much more so than is normal for such a widely dispersed animal species. Modern biology completely contradicts the way we have traditionally created different human races using markers like skin colour and shows that we are one species, certainly culturally different to one another, but with the same genes.

3-SECOND ORIGIN
There is no biological reason for thinking different human races exist; genetically we are almost identical but culturally we display huge diversity.

3-MINUTE DESCENT
The concept of race causes controversy and confusion in equal measure. It's natural to create groups based on perceived differences and we do so based on a huge number of social categories; then we use these labels, like a map, to create a sense of our place within a culturally diverse world. But modern science shows that the idea that there are separate 'human races' simply cannot be sustained in the light of twenty-first-century biology.

RELATED TOPICS
See also
THE NEANDERTHALS
page 22

HOMO SAPIENS
page 24

ANCIENT DNA
page 28

3-SECOND BIOGRAPHIES
JOHANN FRIEDRICH BLUMENBACH
1752–1840
German physician and anthropologist who described five human 'races' based on skull shape

LOUIS AGASSIZ
1807–73
Swiss-American biologist who argued for the existence of many distinct racial groups. He believed that the different human 'races' had distinct origins and his work was widely used to justify slavery in the American South

30-SECOND TEXT
Simon Underdown

There is no such thing as race; we are one species with barely any genetic difference.

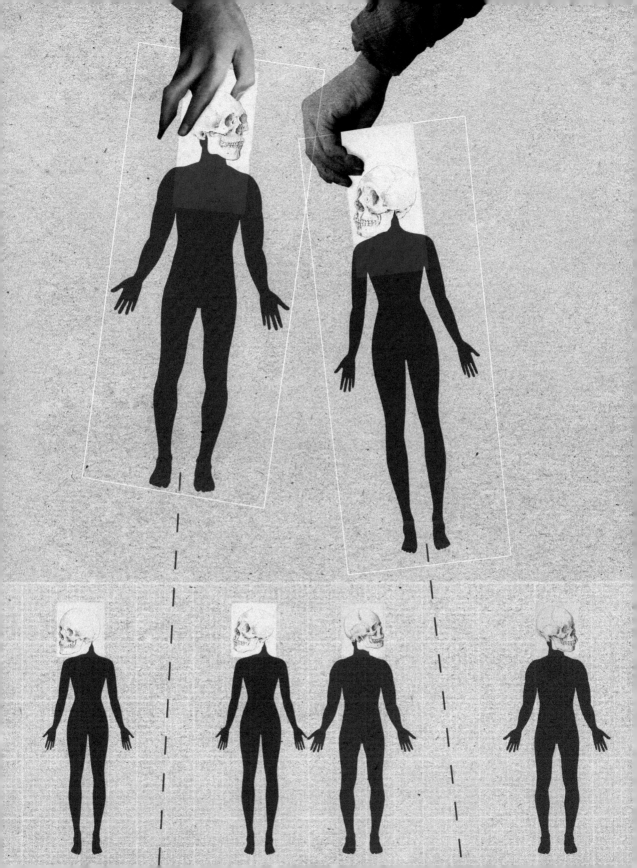

VARIATION

the 30-second anthropology

You can see how everyone is different just by looking around you: eye colour, skin colour, height, weight, nose shape, social awareness and so on. Our species is made up of dozens of populations, each with its own distinctive culture, language and even physical adaptations for its environment. In a relatively short time, after leaving Africa just 100,000 years ago, we have adapted to every environment on the planet, from tropical jungles to the freezing Arctic. The variation in different human populations is astounding. Skin colour is perhaps the most visible difference in populations around the world. Humans in warmer, tropical environments have darker skin (due to more of the pigment melanin) to block the sun's harsh ultraviolet rays. Conversely, in colder environments, people have less melanin in the skin to allow bodies to absorb *more* ultraviolet rays and obtain more vitamin D. People living in high altitudes have developed certain adaptations for this colder, lower-oxygen environment, including larger lung capacities for absorbing more oxygen, and a larger heart to pump the blood around the body more efficiently. Fatty foods are eaten by communities like the Inuit who live in very cold environments. This creates additional fat layers under their skin.

RELATED TOPICS
See also
RACE
page 34

IS ANYONE INDIGENOUS?
page 42

IDENTITY
page 116

3-SECOND ORIGIN
You are unique: every single individual within any species is different; no two individuals are the same.

3-MINUTE DESCENT
Variation is not just limited to our biology. One of our species' ways of surviving in new environments is to develop culture. Today, there are more than 7,000 different recognized cultures – and countless others have been lost in the past. The Maori decorate their faces with elaborate patterns, whereas some Amazonian tribes decorate their faces with piercings. Some communities use animals from their environment as gods to worship. We are one species, but the diversity of populations is magnificent.

3-SECOND BIOGRAPHY
FRANZ BOAS
1858–1942
American pioneer of modern anthropology who argued for cultural relativism – that no one culture can be judged to be better or 'higher' than another

30-SECOND TEXT
Jan Freedman

Variation has been used as the basis for dividing humans for thousands of years. Genetically we display little difference but have developed a massive range of cultural variation.

DISPERSAL & DISTRIBUTION

the 30-second anthropology

Compared to other species,

humans have been very successful in dispersing across the globe. Palaeoanthropologists use environmental clues (such as fossils, tools and artefacts) and genetic evidence (such as DNA from modern or historical populations) to determine when and where hominins travelled. We know, for example, that Europeans and Asians carry 1–4 per cent of Neanderthal DNA through interbreeding between our species. African populations have none, or very little, because their ancestors did not migrate through Eurasia. Which hominins went where and when and how many different species of *Homo* exist is hotly debated. In the 'Out of Africa' hypothesis different *Homo* species coexisted for hundreds of thousands of years, but only ours – descended from a small ancestral group in East Africa 150,000–200,000 years ago – survived. Evidence that Africans are more genetically variable (and therefore older) than populations in Europe and Asia, who have not had so long to diverge, supports this scenario. In the 'multiregional' hypothesis early humans never divided into different species after the first dispersal out of Africa because they continued to interact, have sex and exchange genes. The scientific consensus today largely supports the 'Out of Africa' model.

3-SECOND ORIGIN
Archaic humans began travelling across continents around 2 million years ago when *Homo erectus* dispersed out of Africa into Eurasia.

3-MINUTE DESCENT
One group of hominins dispersed to a rather unusual place: the isolated island of Flores (part of present-day Indonesia). Fossils and stone tools here belong to *Homo floresiensis*, a small-bodied species with a brain unusually small given that the species survived as 'recently' as 50,000 years ago. Making an island your home has consequences, including loss of genetic variation and, for larger mammals including humans, a tendency to reduce in body size due to reduced resources.

RELATED TOPICS
See also
HOMO SAPIENS
page 24

VARIATION
page 36

GLOBALIZATION
page 148

3-SECOND BIOGRAPHIES
REBECCA CANN, MARK STONEKING & ALLAN WILSON
1951–, 1956– & 1934–91
American and New Zealand geneticists whose 1987 study showed that all human populations have a common ancestor in East Africa around 200,000 years ago

30-SECOND TEXT
Djuke Veldhuis

Humans have spread across the world and our journey is recorded in our genes, leaving patterns of variation and adaption in both our biology and culture.

16 December 1901
Born in Philadelphia, Pennsylvania

1922
Meets Ruth Benedict, another student of Franz Boas, who becomes an important teacher, colleague and close confidante throughout her life

1925–1926
Conducts fieldwork in Samoa, concentrating on gender norms and sexuality among adolescent girls. This would result in the best-selling book, *Coming of Age in Samoa*

1931–33
Conducts fieldwork among the Dobu of Papua New Guinea

1935
Publishes *Sex and Temperament in Three Primitive Societies*

8 December 1939
Daughter Mary Catherine Bateson is born. Mary Catherine would go on to become a prominent anthropologist in her own right

1940
Becomes first president of the Society for Applied Anthropology

1942
Becomes associate curator at the American Museum of Natural History, where she continues to work until she retires as full curator emeritus in 1969

1943–45
Works in Washington, D.C., as executive director of the Committee on Food Habits, National Research Council

1962
Begins to write a column for *Redbook* magazine, which she continues to write until her death

15 November 1978
Dies of pancreatic cancer in New York City

MARGARET MEAD

Margaret Mead was born in December 1901 in Philadelphia, Pennsylvania. Her father was a professor of finance at the Wharton School of the University of Pennsylvania, and her mother was a sociologist who studied Italian immigrants. Margaret received a bachelor's degree from Barnard College, New York City, in 1923 and took a master's and PhD at Columbia University, where she studied with Franz Boas and Ruth Benedict.

One of the first women to become prominent in cultural anthropology, Mead was no 'armchair anthropologist' but made multiple trips to the Pacific islands of Samoa, Papua New Guinea and Bali to conduct her fieldwork. 'I learned the value of hard work by working hard', she famously quipped, and it is unquestionable that her hard work paid off, making her one of the most recognizable names in anthropology even today. Strongly influenced by her mentor Franz Boas, Mead had a humanistic belief that anthropology should further the aims of justice, tolerance and mutual understanding.

Mead's ethnographic work on adolescence, gender and sexuality conducted in the 1920s and 1930s in many ways anticipated the attitudes and ideas that would shape feminism and the sexual liberation movement of the 1960s. Mead argued that a person's culture and not her biology determined her limits and freedom in life. She found that in societies with comparatively relaxed attitudes about adolescent premarital sexuality activity, like Samoa, transitions to adulthood were less fraught than in the West. Mead's Samoan interlocutors were much more than 'noble savages' or nameless test subjects; they spoke and moved and lived their lives with a vivid humanity that allowed readers to feel a closeness to them, rare in scientific writing. Mead's ethnography held a mirror up to the West, pushing readers to question their own assumptions about human nature.

Through her work for the US government during the Second World War and for UNESCO and the World Health Organization after, Mead continued to bring anthropology into public life. She even wrote an advice column in *Redbook* magazine, in which she answered questions on everything from baseball to hairstyles. Her lasting legacy to anthropologists is the inspiration to work towards social betterment while respecting the value of cultural commitments and traditions.

Jason Danely

IS ANYONE INDIGENOUS?

the 30-second anthropology

Humans have a profound relationship with where they are from. Home is central to how we think about our identity and create ideas about our history. Just as we use labels to manage our relationships with other people, our sense of identity is intrinsically tied to concepts of where we come from. But our needs and curiosity have pushed us across the globe. All humans living today can trace their roots to a population who lived in East Africa around 200,000 years ago. When, around 100,000 years later, our ancestors began to expand beyond Africa they established populations across the globe. These original, founding inhabitants of a region are the indigenous people, with unique social and cultural traditions and strong ties to the land they inhabit, which are passed down to their descendants. But the survival of these cultures through subsequent generations can be threatened by newcomers, whose own systems and beliefs come to dominate, often by force. From the European colonization of the Americas in the fifteenth and sixteenth centuries through to the growth of nationalism and colonialism in the eighteenth and nineteenth centuries, the rights of indigenous people have also clashed violently with economic imperatives. Sadly we have yet to reconcile our shared evolutionary history with the bottom dollar.

3-SECOND ORIGIN
The human species shares one ancestral location in East Africa but has made the world our home.

3-MINUTE DESCENT
The speed and ease with which we can traverse the globe has had a profound impact on our species. The internet allows us to share ideas and trends as quickly as they are thought of. Indigenous cultures and ideas are facing an unprecedented level of influence, which threatens to dilute thousands of years of cultural diversity and concepts of identity.

RELATED TOPICS
See also
AFRICA
page 44

ASIA
page 46

EUROPE
page 48

3-SECOND BIOGRAPHIES
LOUIS & MARY LEAKEY
1903–72 & 1913–96
Kenyan and British husband and wife palaeoanthropologists who were pioneers of the study of human evolution in Africa

30-SECOND TEXT
Jan Freedman

Arguably all humans outside of Africa are relatively recent arrivals in Europe, Asia, America and Australasia.

AFRICA

the 30-second anthropology

Africa is home to around 3,000 different groups of people: what is astonishing is that each group is more genetically different from the others than a European person is from an Asian person. Despite the large internal genetic diversity, on the outside all native Africans share a dark skin colour; a result of the same pigments that give colour to our eyes and hair: melanin. More melanin in our skin gives it a darker colour; an enormous advantage in warmer climates because the more melanin, the more protection against skin cancer. The lighter skin colour of many other populations around the world is a result of our bodies needing to obtain more vitamin D from the sun, which is not as strong as it is in Africa. Each of these 3,000 African groups has its own distinctive culture: a unique identity for that tribe. For example, a man from the Lobola tribe, in Southern Africa, wanting to marry must pay for his bride, whereas Wodaabe men in Central Africa must win the girl by showing off their skills in dancing. Africa is unique. There are many cultures that have not changed in thousands of years, with groups foraging for food across the land, forming territories as they go.

RELATED TOPIC
See also
RACE
page 34

3-SECOND ORIGIN
Our species was born in Africa: no matter where you live in the world today, you can trace your ancestors back to the cradle of humankind.

3-MINUTE DESCENT
The expansion of other cultures resulted in kingdoms being formed in Africa, to try to defend the people from invaders. However, it wasn't until the 1800s that Europeans claimed their own parts of Africa and soon after, in 1913, created boundaries for 40 African states – becoming the 54 countries we know today. It was only from the 1950s onwards that these countries began to gain their independence.

3-SECOND BIOGRAPHIES
NELSON MANDELA
1918–2013
In 1994, Mandela was the first black South African president. He fought against racism in the country and focused on human rights. Mandela was, and still is, an inspirational figure in recent African history

RICHARD & MEAVE LEAKEY
1944– & 1942–
A husband and wife team who made significant discoveries to help our understanding of the human family tree

30-SECOND TEXT
Jan Freedman

Africa is the birthplace of our species and is home to the widest and oldest range of human genetic diversity.

ASIA

the 30-second anthropology

The main reason for the success of the human race is our ability to adapt to any type of environment. In Asia we have managed to survive and thrive in an incredible array of habitats, including mountains, deserts, jungles and coastal regions. People have adapted to live in the hotter Middle East with leaner bodies and a darker skin, whereas people living in the extremely high and cold Tibetan plateau have much larger lungs to enable more oxygen to reach their blood. Asia is a fruitful and rich land to live in, and for millennia humans have been at home here. Archaeological evidence shows one of the world's oldest civilizations was in China, around 9,000 years ago, with the building of temples, and the development of religion and rituals following soon after. Farming the land with rice crops and animals provided a means of sustaining large groups of people, as it still does today. Large populations need structure and leadership, and this can be seen in the First Dynasty around 4,000 years ago. Clay tablets dating to roughly 5,000 years ago, discovered in the ancient city of Sumer in present-day Iraq, show the earliest evidence of writing. Religion has been a strong part of the culture of Asia, with the birth there of Judaism, Christianity and Islam in the Middle East, Buddhism in Nepal, Hinduism in India, and many others.

3-SECOND ORIGIN
With over 14 different religions, 18 different languages and a plethora of different customs and cultures, people living in Asia are more diverse than anywhere else in the world.

3-MINUTE DESCENT
It was only relatively recently that the West had a large influence on Asia. The Second World War marked the end of most of the old cultural ways. It also marked the power and ignorance of our species: the dropping of an atomic bomb on Hiroshima was not only a changing moment for Japan, but also for our whole planet and the ease with which we can destroy it.

RELATED TOPICS
See also
RACE
page 34

RELIGION & BELIEF
page 114

3-SECOND BIOGRAPHIES
GENGHIS KHAN
1162–1227
Founder and ruler of the Mongol Empire, known for running brutal conquering campaigns

MAHATMA GANDHI
1869–1948
Indian nationalist leader and advocate of non-violent protest

30-SECOND TEXT
Jan Freedman

A remarkably rich and diverse source of human culture for thousands of years, Asia's future will be shaped by its economic super powers.

EUROPE

the 30-second anthropology

The first human species to

colonize Europe was *Homo erectus* 1.8 million years ago in Georgia, followed later by the Neanderthals, who then disappeared around 20–30,000 years ago. Our own species *Homo sapiens* began to appear in Europe after 50,000 years ago. After the end of the Ice Age 12,000 years ago we started creating more permanent settlements that began as villages and grew into the towns, cities and mega-conurbations that exist today. The Roman Empire has left a footprint that shapes many of the landscapes, laws and traditions that characterize modern Europe and is often held up as a model of civilization against the so-called 'Dark Ages' when Roman influence moved to the east. The Medieval period in Europe was characterized by power struggles that carved out dozens of small kingdoms. Not until the Renaissance, which paved the way for the Enlightenment, do we start to see the picture of modern Europe emerging. While arguably a 'young' human continent, Europe displays the full range of human cultural complexity, achievement and capacity for self-destruction. Modern Europe in the form of the EU has been shaped by the history of our ancestors – a perfect reflection of what anthropology seeks to understand.

3-SECOND ORIGIN
The Roman Empire created the template for European empires both at home and abroad and Latin remains the root of many modern European languages.

3-MINUTE DESCENT
Although a relatively small land mass, Europe has driven and dictated the development of global ideas. The best/worst example is the Second World War. The crumbling of the old political system based on elites triggered the First World War, which in turn precipitated the rise of Fascism and culminated in the Holocaust – the darkest expression of human evil. The European Union was born from the desire to create peaceful relationships and strong trade partnerships between countries.

RELATED TOPICS
See also
THE NEANDERTHALS
page 22

HOMO SAPIENS
page 24

3-SECOND BIOGRAPHIES
ARISTOTLE
384–322 BCE
Greek philosopher and scientist who was the first great thinker in Europe, who studied geology, physics, biology, medicine and psychology

PAUL-HENRI SPAAK
1899–1972
Belgian politician who led the intergovernment committee in the early 1950s, which led to the birth of the European Economic Community, later to become the European Union

30-SECOND TEXT
Jan Freedman

From ancient Rome to the modern day, the political and financial power of Europe has shaped human trade, political and social values.

THE AMERICAS

the 30-second anthropology

3-SECOND ORIGIN
North America was first colonized 20,000 years ago and today is one of the most multicultural places on the planet.

3-MINUTE DESCENT
After the arrival of the Europeans, all the cultures in North and South America were changed forever. The Spanish came to South America in the early 1500s in search of gold, but brought with them warfare and disease. Soon after, many European countries sent boats full of people to North America to settle, resulting in severe conflict with the native Americans and thousands being killed.

The United States of America

is one of the most powerful countries in the world. Yet modern North and South America is a relatively recent development, only coming into being after they were re-colonized in the seventeenth and eighteenth centuries. The first groups of people reached North America around 20,000 years ago after trekking across Siberia, and quickly spread south, colonizing the large landmass. The cultures that developed were dramatically unalike, reflecting the extremely different environments humans lived in. In North America, the first evidence of culture is seen in fine flint points, known as the Clovis culture. After just a few thousand years, as people spread new cultures emerged and the Clovis vanished. North American people lived off the land, with groups owning a piece of land and having one tribal leader. In contrast, the more temperate climates with a richer variety of plants and animals in South America allowed people to live together in large complex groups. These groups developed social structures, writing, architecture and farming, marking the first civilizations on the continent. The Aztecs (North Mexico), Mayans (Middle Mexico) and Incas (Peru) are the most well known, although there were dozens of other smaller cultures across the large landmass.

RELATED TOPIC
See also
RACE
page 34

3-SECOND BIOGRAPHIES
MOCTEZUMA II
c. 1466–1520
Ruler of the Aztec Empire at its greatest size, who was killed by Spanish conquistadors

THOMAS JEFFERSON
1743–1826
One of America's founding fathers who wrote the Declaration of Independence and became America's third president

MARTIN LUTHER KING
1929–1968
A leader in the civil rights movement using non-violent marches against racial inequality, poverty and the Vietnam War. King was assassinated in 1968

30-SECOND TEXT
Jan Freedman

The Clovis in the north and the Aztecs and Mayans in the south were among the many original cultures to populate the Americas.

AUSTRALASIA

the 30-second anthropology

3-SECOND ORIGIN
Outside of Africa, the
Aboriginal Australians are
the oldest living population
of humans in the world.

3-MINUTE DESCENT
In the late 1700s to
mid-1800s, more than
160,000 European convicts
were transported to
Australia. The attraction
of gold and land also
brought several thousand
new settlers to Australia,
having a devastating
impact on the native
Aboriginal people as they
lost their way of life. Today
many Aboriginal people
have adapted to modern
Western culture, but this
has had a knock-on effect
to their way of life: their
connection with nature is
slowly disappearing.

Around 50,000 years ago, a drier climate helped the first people to arrive on Australia. Rock paintings and carvings as old as 40,000 years capture the unique local fauna that has long since vanished and these are still visited by Aboriginal people today, with the ancient art holding many different meanings: symbols to old legends, or connections to old dreams. The large island of nearby Papua New Guinea was colonized around 40,000 years ago and today boasts more than 1,000 different tribes with more than 1,000 different languages – and it is estimated that there are at least 40 tribes still to be discovered there. New Zealand was only colonized around 800 years ago by Polynesian sailors. Here, the new people to New Zealand developed their own culture: the Māori used bird feathers to decorate their clothing, marking their status; and storytelling was performed through their unique, and now famous, *kapa haka* dance. Although several ships had landed on the coast of Australia, it was claimed as British territory by Captain James Cook in 1770. New settlers brought with them new disease and warfare, killing thousands of the native Aboriginal people and resulting in the loss of dozens of cultures. Hidden in the dense jungles, the native populations of Papua New Guinea were relatively untouched.

RELATED TOPIC
See also
RACE
page 34

3-SECOND BIOGRAPHIES
CAPTAIN JAMES COOK
1728–1779
The first person to navigate
and map Australia and New
Zealand, Cook opened up
these new lands for European
colonization. After being alone
for around 50,000 years,
the Australian Aboriginal
populations were badly
affected

EDITH COWAN
1861–1932
The first woman elected to the
Australian parliament, Cowan
had a large influence on
women's rights in Australia
in the late 1800s and early
1900s, including successfully
campaigning for women to be
allowed to vote

30-SECOND TEXT
Jan Freedman

Nineteenth-century colonial European ambitions had a devastating impact on indigenous cultures in Australasia.

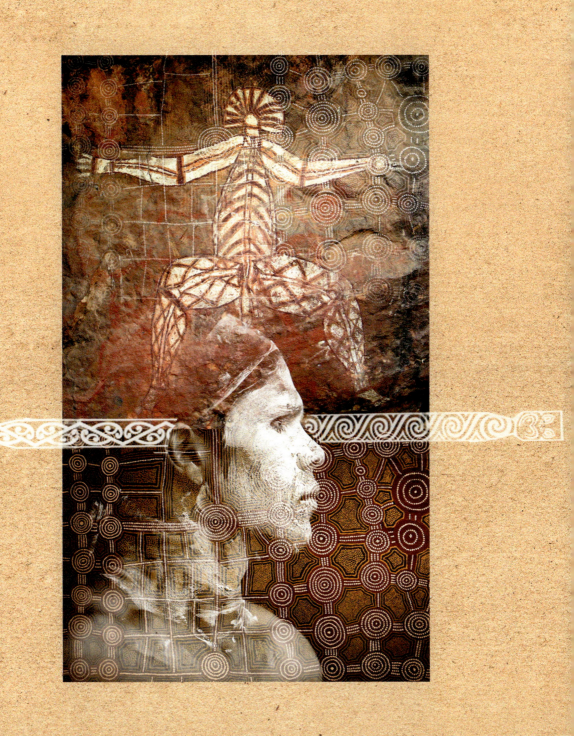

MATERIALS

archaeometallurgy The analysis and study of archaeological metals and how they were made in the past.

archaeometry An umbrella term that describes the use and application of dating techniques to archaeological material.

biological anthropology The branch of anthropology that explores human biology using an evolutionary perspective.

Bronze Age The Bronze Age is the period of human history that typically sees the use of bronze metal, early writing and increased urbanization. In the Middle East it dates from around 3300–1200 BCE and in Europe from 3200–600 BCE.

Chalcolithic period The period immediately preceding the Bronze Age; it is seen as a link between the Neolithic and the Bronze Age and sees the widespread use of copper in tool making.

complex societies A term in anthropology that refers to any human grouping that has specialized division of activities and that is tightly regulated by laws and customs.

cultural anthropology The study of cultural variation in human groups that typically makes use of participant observation and extended field study.

cultural relativism A theory in social anthropology developed by Franz Boas that argues that beliefs can only be understood in the context they come from.

Faynan Region in southern Jordan that is home to some of the earliest complex human societies known to archaeology.

genetic engineering In the strict sense, the use of biotechnology to directly alter the genome of an organism. In reality, humans have been 'engineering' the genomes of plants and animals for thousands of years through selective breeding.

holistic Dealing with something as a whole, not just a part. Social anthropologists continue to argue over the holistic nature of the subject. One camp suggests that since anthropology is concerned with all aspects of humanity it is inherently holistic, while opponents to this view see this as an attempt to impose scientific thinking.

Holocene period The current geological epoch. This followed the Pleistocene and began around 11,700 years ago. Some researchers argue that the Holocene has ended and we are now in the Anthropocene (triggered by human climate change).

Homo sapiens Our own species name, which means 'wise man'. All living humans today can trace our ancestry back to East Africa around 200,000 years ago.

indigenous A term used to describe the earliest inhabitants of a region and their living descendants.

linguistic anthropology The study of the role of language and its use on human social structure and interaction.

Mesopotamia Traditionally viewed as one of the cradles of humanity and situated in modern-day Iraq. Human activity in the area dates back almost 10,000 years and is home to the earliest known writing – Sumerian cuneiform.

metallurgy Branch of materials science that examines the traits and behaviours of metals.

Neolithic period Beginning in the Middle East around 10,000 years ago, this period saw the development of farming and the use of secondary products from livestock such as skins, milk and other materials.

Pleistocene Geological epoch between aproximately 2.6 million and 11,700 years ago.

CLAY

the 30-second anthropology

Malleable and, once dried or

fired, resistant, clay has been used since the late Pleistocene era (around 125,000 years ago) for containers both large and small: as pottery and – in the form of adobe, brick and plaster – for building. These uses developed independently in different regions of the world. The earliest pottery was made c. 16,000 years ago in East Asia, c. 12,000 years ago in North Africa and c. 7,500 years ago in the Amazon Basin. Pottery extends the scope of culinary and subsistence practices through its role in storing, preparing and cooking food and in biochemical processes such as fermentation. Prior to the use of glass, metal and plastic containers, it was in pottery vessels that foodstuffs were transported, as seen in the amphoras used for long-distance olive oil trade in the Roman empire. Building with clay was a separate innovation to potting, but the principle, in terms of creating containers, is similar. Adobe (mud/clay) and mud-brick construction is found throughout the world. The early cities of the ancient Near East, Indus Valley and East Asia rose from mud-bricks. Ceramic (fired) building materials – such as brick and tile – delivered durability and potentially infinite modular building.

3-SECOND ORIGIN
The malleability of clay has made it an ideal medium for containers large and small, for making spaces to live in and pots to cook with.

3-MINUTE DESCENT
Clay is good to think with – metaphors of shaping and moulding link clay with the socialization of the body and mind. People saw that containers with mouths, necks, bodies and feet formed and hardened; that they had lives of usage and breakage. Across different cultures, pots are identified as having the qualities of people.

RELATED TOPICS
See also
TOOLS
page 18

FIRE
page 20

ART & ARTEFACT
page 90

30-SECOND TEXT
Joshua Pollard

Humans have used clay for millennia, from making small containers to building homes and temples.

9 July 1858
Born in Minden, Germany, into a liberal Jewish family

1881
Obtains a doctorate from Kiel University on the refraction of light in sea water

1883
Returns to geography and makes a first research trip to study the Inuit in Baffin Bay, Canada

1886
Obtains thesis on his northern research

1887
Emigrates to the United States

1888
Takes position at Clark University

1892
Resigns from Clark University

1896
Appointed assistant curator at the American Museum of Natural History; also lectures at Columbia University

1899
Appointed professor of anthropology at Columbia University, becomes head of department

1905
Resigns from the museum

21 December 1942
Dies in New York City

FRANZ BOAS

Franz Boas is regarded as the founder of professional anthropology in the United States. Born in Germany, he studied physics and geography at Heidelberg and Bonn but after his doctorate turned more towards geography, then anthropology, choosing as his area of research the indigenous peoples of the North. This became a lifelong interest.

Boas was born to a Jewish family and, as anti-Semitism was becoming ever more evident in Germany, emigrated to the United States in 1887. He was a writer on the journal *Science*, then took a position at Clark University, before consolidating his career, first as curator at the American Natural History Museum, then at Columbia University, where he remained until his death in 1942. Throughout this time, he was a highly effective teacher, with many of his pupils, such as Alfred Kroeber, becoming notable anthropologists.

Boas brought with him from Europe a holistic view of anthropology, and throughout his career combined an interest in biological, linguistic and cultural anthropology. He drew on all these fields to stress his understanding of anthropology as a study that embraced cultural relativism and rejected racism. He wrote widely on these themes – in general terms in *The Mind of Primitive Man* (1911), as well as more specifically, such as showing how influential the environment was in changing the cranial dimensions of migrants to the United States.

Deeply convinced of the moral purpose of anthropology, he denounced those who permitted their work or their profession to be used as a cover by governmental agencies . This sometimes combative, but meticulous and dedicated professional approach was seminal in the development of anthropology in the United States. Among many other professional roles, he became president of the American Anthropological Association in 1907.

Yet Boas was always an internationalist: he tried to start a field school in Mexico and kept up a wide-ranging correspondence and interaction with colleagues in Europe. He wanted to establish a framework to address intellectual problems while ensuring anthropology was free from outside influence. His death in the University Faculty Club in December 1942 came just after he had given a powerful denunciation of racism.

David Shankland

BRONZE AGE METALLURGY

the 30-second anthropology

RELATED TOPICS
See also
TOOLS
page 18

INDUSTRY & MINING
page 64

3-SECOND ORIGIN
From small-scale use in the Chalcolithic period, copper developed to become a central pillar of Bronze Age civilization.

3-MINUTE DESCENT
Early copper smelting was labour-intensive: place a clay bowl (crucible) containing copper ore in a bed of burning charcoal; add more burning charcoal into the crucible with the ore, and add air using a blowpipe to raise the temperature to 1,084°C (1,983°F); maintain this heat until the ore becomes small metallic particles (prills). Once cooled, separate the prills and combine with the results of other crucible smelts; melt to form a pool of liquid copper.

Imagine a world without metal. Modern civilization has been built on our ability to take raw minerals and turn them into metal. In terms of the history of humanity this is a fairly recent phenomenon. Most of our time on Earth as *Homo sapiens* (from about 200,000 years ago) was spent using simple stone, bone and wooden tools. Then c. 7,000 years ago humans discovered that fire could be used to transform blue/green minerals into shiny metal objects, a process that must have seemed magical. Although the origins of metallurgy are obscure and highly debated, what is clear from the archaeological record is that during the period immediately preceding the Bronze Age humans began to use these rare and highly prized copper objects as markers of social status. At the beginning of the Bronze Age (c. 3500 BCE) in what is now the Middle East, the evolution of complex societies was to a large degree built on the ability to create and control copper production. Metal at this time became central to human societies, transitioning from being a marker of status to become a commodity used to create tools and objects of great beauty. All early civilizations from ancient Egypt to Mesopotamia sought to acquire copper (and later silver and gold) as a basis of the creation of wealth and power.

3-SECOND BIOGRAPHIES
BENO ROTHENBERG
1914–2012
German archaeometallurgist who pioneered a multi-disciplinary approach that combined archaeological investigation with science-based approaches (later known as archaeometry)

RONALD F. TYLECOTE
1916–90
British archaeologist/metallurgist generally recognized as the founder of archaeometallurgy

30-SECOND TEXT
Russell Adams

The manipulation of bronze metal marked the end of the stone age, 3 million years of hominin and human industry.

INDUSTRY & MINING

the 30-second anthropology

The origins of mining date at

least to the Neolithic period, when humans began to extract brightly coloured minerals (such as the blue/green chrysocolla) for beads and for colourants. By the Chalcolithic period miners had progressed to larger-scale open-cast exploration for extracting ores for smelting and then to random tunnelling, as seen at Timna (Israel). In the early Bronze Age (c. 2800 BCE) people developed shaft and gallery mining with the aim of expanding the scale of ore extraction. Vertical mine shafts connected with horizontal galleries that followed ore beds; in many cases waste mining rock was left in the mine to provide support to prevent the collapse of galleries. The advance of mining technology reflected the growing need for metals in early complex societies and is mirrored by other advances in technology, which becomes more 'industrial' at this time; this is certainly true of smelting and fabrication of copper as seen at Faynan (Jordan), where large smelters lined the windward side of high hills to use natural draft to smelt copper ore, and at Khirbat Hamra Ifdan (also in Jordan), where data from the earliest recorded 'factory' (c. 2600 BCE) indicates an almost assembly-line process of refining, casting and refinishing copper objects alongside the production of copper ingots for trade.

RELATED TOPICS
See also
BRONZE AGE METALLURGY
page 62

TRADE
page 100

3-SECOND ORIGIN
Complex, class-based societies developed on the back of industrialization, as elites sought to acquire rare and specialized products to enhance their wealth and status.

3-MINUTE DESCENT
Industrialization is one of the hallmarks of the emergence of complex societies during the fourth and third millenniums BCE. In addition to mining and metallurgical production, another area of ancient industry included textile production. In ancient Mesopotamia, evidence suggests this textile production occurred in large complexes and was accompanied by the introduction of slaves. These textiles created opportunities to advance long-distance trade, which in turn led to the emergence of elite classes.

3-SECOND BIOGRAPHY
GERD WEISGERBER
1938–2010
German mining archaeologist who, through extensive work in Europe and the Middle East (Oman, Israel, Jordan and Iran), developed this field into a scientific subdiscipline of archaeology

30-SECOND TEXT
Russell Adams

From its origins in the stone age, mining led to the development of industry on an enormous scale.

CRAFT

the 30-second anthropology

Craft implies making, but making with skill, attentiveness and a certain respect for received ways of proceeding. It is different from the routine, subsistence-based production of things. Historians hypothesize that craft specialization – allowing certain individuals or groups of individuals to devote their energy to the production of specialized goods such as beads, metalwork and weaponry – emerged in the early Holocene period (c. 12,000 years ago) when the display of material goods began to signify position and identity. The ability to create items of value or power (both secular and cosmological) became significant and craft production began to be heavily controlled. Carving in Māori culture was considered a sacred act. In medieval Europe, craftsmen operated within guilds, self-regulated and often secretive. Yet it is a mistake to equate craft just with non- or pre-industrial worlds. Craft survives and thrives in industrialized environments, whether as a hobby in the West or through its capacity to rework mass-produced things. In the Global South, recycled wire and drinks cans become baskets and toys for sale to augment subsistence economies. The *materiel* of the First World War – shell and bullet cases – was transformed into trench art, a process that inscribed meaning and memory onto alienated things.

3-SECOND ORIGIN
Craft may be equated with specialized and skilled modes of making; in an industrial world it connects people to the values of personalized labour.

3-MINUTE DESCENT
The learning of craft skills requires observation, mimicry and instruction. Where those skills are intricate or highly valued a system of apprenticeship may be required. For would-be master carvers in the Massim region of Papua New Guinea, the process involves not just learning to carve, but also following strict food taboos and training in magic to allow clear thought.

RELATED TOPICS
See also
TOOLS
page 18

INDUSTRY & MINING
page 64

ART & ARTEFACT
page 90

30-SECOND TEXT
Joshua Pollard

A crafted object – whether carved in stone or made from recycled materials – reflects the skill of its maker.

DISCOVERIES

the 30-second anthropology

To be human is to be inquisitive and adaptive, to seek material solutions to problems and to exploit opportunities. It is within a melting pot of necessity, availability (of materials, skills and the right environment) and sometimes serendipity that discovery occurs. Even laboratory-based science discovery can be a 'messy' practice in which social context and technical content shape each other and invention need not always follow design: take the discovery of penicillin, for example, by Alexander Fleming in 1928. There is also the matter of societal acceptance. Often the biggest obstacle to innovation can be social rather than technical: see, for example, the slow uptake of the earliest forms of metallurgy in prehistoric Europe, the rejection of electric cars in the mid twentieth-century United States or current resistance to genetic engineering. In the industrialized West, at least, there is a fixation with discovery. It is easy to envisage narratives of linear progress stretching from prehistory to the present – the discovery of farming, of writing, of mechanics, of powered flight, computing, molecular engineering – and so on. But this narrative is particular and the Eurasian record has, on a global canvas, been peculiar.

30-SECOND TEXT
Joshua Pollard

Curiosity is not unique to humans, but our ability to apply it to problems is profound. We have harnessed our ability to discover and innovate to shape the pattern of our evolution.

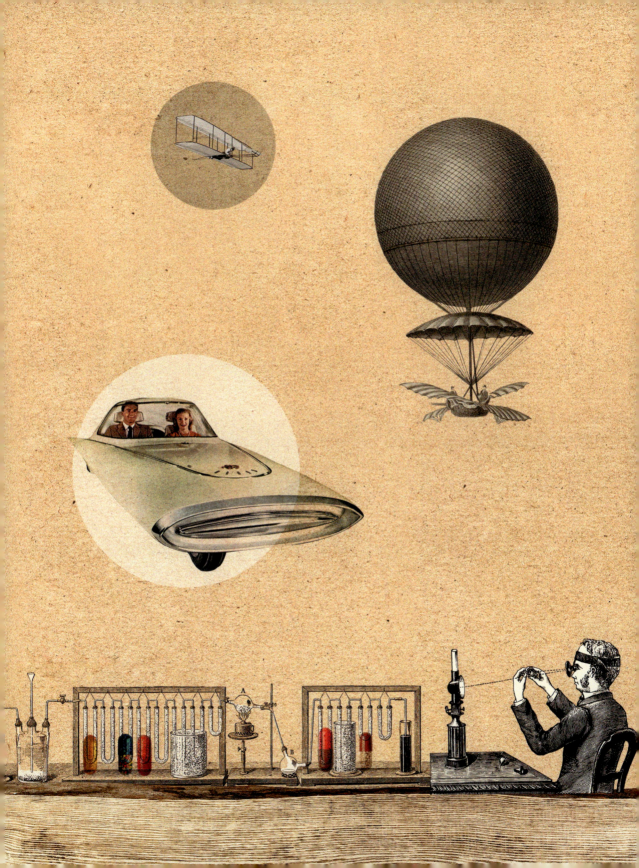

SOCIALIZATION & COMMUNICATION

Aztecs A cultural group found in Central Mexico between the fourteenth and sixteenth centuries. Known mostly from archaeological evidence and the often lurid accounts written by Spanish colonialists.

communicative competence Describes a language-user's ability to not only understand the grammar and syntax of a language but also their social knowledge of when and how to use words.

creole A language that has naturally developed from a combination of other languages. Creoles have fully developed systems of grammar and syntax.

ethnography The systematic social-cultural study of people, often referring to the written account of such research.

evolutionary psychology Branch of anthropology that focuses on the relationship between the human evolutionary process and psychological traits. Many proponents of evolutionary psychology argue that how humans think today was shaped by the experiences of our ancestors.

genetically modified (GM) food The use of genetic engineering to change the DNA of crops to increase productivity and disease resistance. While GM can be thought of as a more technologically advanced form of selective breeding, the manipulation of DNA offers much greater control.

grammar The structural rules of a language that control how words are used so that the language makes sense.

kamikaze pilots Pilots who flew suicide missions against the ships of the Allied forces during the latter stages of the Second World War. In Japan kamikaze pilots were thought of as continuers of the Samurai Bushido tradition.

linguistic relativity A concept in linguistic anthropology that argues the structure of a language directly influences the speaker's thought processes.

Mesolithic period Also known as the Epipalaeolithic, an archaeological term that describes stone tool forms used from 20,000 years ago until around the end of the Pleistocene.

Middle Palaeolithic Archaeological period from around 300,000 to 30,000 years ago. In Europe it is closely associated with the Neanderthals and Mousterian stone tools. It is during this period that *Homo sapiens* began to expand out of Africa some time around 100,000 years ago.

nucleation Process that describes how human settlements tend to develop in increasing size and density.

Palaeolithic period Archaeological period traditionally covering the use of stone tools from 2.6 million years ago until the end of the Pleistocene. With the discovery of the Lomekwian stone tools from 3.3 million years ago, the Palaeolithic (as a non-geological term) can be pushed back in time.

pidgin A language that develops from two or more unrelated languages as a means of simplified communication, generally without formal grammatical rules and conventions.

primatology An umbrella term to cover a diverse range of primate studies, including behaviour and conservation.

prosocial Used to describe voluntary behaviours that are for the benefit of others, such as sharing, cooperation and obeying the rules that govern a society.

sedentism Literally staying in one place. In biological anthropology it describes the long-term process of changing from a mobile hunter-gatherer lifestyle to a generally agriculturally focused one. In social anthropology it refers to any population that has lived in one place for a long time.

semantics The study of the meanings of words and how they are used.

semiotics The study of signs and symbols and how they have been developed over time.

social anthropology Branch of anthropology that studies human societies and culture.

speech community A loosely defined term that describes a group of people who use a language in a particular way and is often used as a way of defining group identity.

DOMESTICATION

the 30-second anthropology

The first clear evidence of plant and animal domestication dates to 10,000–8000 BCE, when the mobile hunter-gatherer lifestyle gave way to temporary cultivation (horticulture) and then intensive agriculture, in which fields were permanently maintained. This period is called the 'Neolithic Revolution' and occurred independently at different times in different parts of the world. The first evidence comes from the Near East, with signs of the domestication of dogs (tamed wolves) in what is now northern Israel c. 10,000 BCE. It was followed there by the domestication of plants (wheat, oats, rye, barley), sheep and goats around 8000 BCE. The same trend was seen later in East Asia and Africa and finally in the Americas. One consequence of the Neolithic Revolution was that it allowed people to live in one place; this sedentism may have boosted population growth because it allowed people to reduce the time between childbirths – and therefore fertility increased. Ultimately the development of agriculture was a gradual transformation over thousands of years. Population increases, developments in technology (for example, the spindle and loom) and elaboration of material possessions (such as textiles and pottery) set the stage for the first cities, which appeared in the Near East around c. 3500 BCE.

RELATED TOPICS
See also
TOOLS
page 18

FIRE
page 20

GENETIC ENGINEERING
page 142

3-SECOND BIOGRAPHIES
NIKOLAI IVANOVICH VAVILOV
1887–1943
Russian botanist and geneticist who identified the centres of origin of a variety of crops

RACHEL CARSON
1907–64
American marine biologist, conservationist and author whose book *Silent Spring* (1962) warned of the harmful effects of pesticides and advanced the global environmental movement

30-SECOND TEXT
Djuke Veldhuis

Humans have been domesticating plants and animals to suit their needs for thousands of years.

3-SECOND ORIGIN
The cultivation and domestication of plants and animals began independently in different parts of the world and served as a precursor for large-scale sedentary human civilizations.

3-MINUTE DESCENT
In the twentieth century industrial-scale agriculture was made possible by mechanization and the development of synthetic fertilizers to increase crop yields. The twenty-first century sees the next 'revolution': genetically modified (GM) food. Technically GM has existed since humans started selective breeding for traits – and therefore genes. But the ability to directly modify genes, to make crops resistant to viruses for example, could save people from starvation. Concerns remain about GM safety.

SETTLEMENT

the 30-second anthropology

Although hunter-gatherers in the Palaeolithic and Mesolithic periods built temporary shelters, the first permanent settlements appeared only in the Neolithic period, when people started farming and could secure the food supply to stay put for any length of time. From then on the number, diversity and size of permanent settlements increased. From the fourth millennium BCE, towns emerged, perhaps first at Uruk in Mesopotamia, along with a new form of political organization, the state, which would eventually come to dominate the world. The relationship between urbanism and the state was crucial to the development of later settlement patterns. Trade, conquest and imperialism, especially the rise of the Roman Empire, took urbanism into new geographical areas and enabled the growth of vast cities, such as first-century Rome or sixth-century Constantinople (modern Istanbul). Great cities became the centres of international trade; the rise of industrial economies and globalization fuelled further increases in the number, scale and interconnectedness of urban communities around the world. Nevertheless, only in the past century has a shift occurred to the majority of the world population living in urban, rather than rural, settings.

RELATED TOPICS
See also
HOMO SAPIENS
page 24

TRADE
page 100

GLOBALIZATION
page 148

3-SECOND ORIGIN
Building settlements creates a framework for everyday life. But for most of human history people moved around the landscape rather than settling in any one place.

3-MINUTE DESCENT
The main constraints on settlement size can be how information is exchanged and processed, means of communication (including travel) and environment. As information and communication methods accelerate, will the rate of settlement-nucleation accelerate also, or will environmental constraints limit this? Presumably, there is a maximum size beyond which urban growth is no longer sustainable, but how can that threshold be identified and how close are the largest cities of the twenty-first century to it?

3-SECOND BIOGRAPHIES
CONSTANTINE THE GREAT
C. 272–337 CE
Roman emperor who refounded the Greek trading colony of Byzantium as the imperial city of Constantinople, capital of the Roman Empire for more than 1,000 years

WILLIAM KENNETT LOFTUS
1820–58
English geologist and archaeologist who discovered and excavated the ancient Sumerian city of Uruk in 1849

30-SECOND TEXT
Ken Dark

The idea of home is so central to being human, yet permanent human settlements only started to develop from around 12,000 years ago.

7 April 1884
Born in Krakow, Poland, to a cultured, academic family

1908
Receives his doctorate in science and philosophy from the Jagiellonian University, Krakow

1910
Attends courses at the London School of Economics (LSE), becoming a graduate student there in 1913

1914
Goes to Australia as secretary to Section H of the British Association for the Advancement of Science

1914–18
Conducts fieldwork in Papua New Guinea, notably in the Trobriand Islands from 1916 onwards

1922
Publishes *Argonauts of the Western Pacific*

1923
Returns to the LSE as a lecturer in anthropology

1927
Becomes a professor of anthropology at the LSE

1938
Departs for the United States on sabbatical

1939
Becomes visiting professor at Yale University

1942
Appointed professor of anthropology at Yale University

16 May 1942
Dies of a heart attack

BRONISLAW MALINOWSKI

Bronislaw Malinowski had

a profound influence in shaping modern anthropology just as it was beginning to become established as a university subject in Britain. Polish by birth, he obtained a PhD in the Philosophy of Science in Krakow, then – attracted to anthropology – he enrolled as a student at the London School of Economics.

A supremely gifted fieldworker, Malinowski developed his ideas in Papua New Guinea. In 1914 he set off there to attend the British Association for the Advancement of Science meeting. However, following the outbreak of the First World War, he could not return to Europe because he was an Austrian subject and as such an enemy of Britain. He did research in the Trobriand Islands throughout the war and, once back in London, ran a postgraduate seminar that attracted students from around the world.

Malinowski insisted upon the importance of empirical fieldwork in a specific community, conducted in the language of the peoples being studied. He emphasized that rather than seek historical continuities we should understand the way that present-day concerns dominate our understanding of the past. Controversially, he propounded a form of functionalism – the idea

that all parts of society are interconnected – that regarded social institutions as being rooted in biological needs. This approach was explained in volumes devoted to his Trobriand researches, and epitomized by his book *Argonauts of the Western Pacific* (1922).

Malinowski was a gifted teacher, questioning and debating with his students as well as sharing his latest thoughts and ideas. Many who attended his seminars went on to occupy leading positions in anthropology, notably Raymond Firth, who took over Malinowski's chair at the LSE, Meyer Fortes, who went to the University of Cambridge and Edward Evans-Pritchard, who became social anthropology professor at the University of Oxford.

Historians of anthropology often call Malinowski's impact revolutionary. This is partly true. He reshaped anthropology, creating a method that could be easily taught and followed – in theory at least. Yet his conception of functionalism was not widely taken up. It is best to see him as one of the founders – another being Alfred Radcliffe-Brown – of the social anthropology that came to dominate in the UK and in Europe during the second half of the twentieth century.

David Shankland

LINGUISTICS

the 30-second anthropology

Every human society has a
language. All language users depend on the
same basic cognitive capacities, yet the range
of linguistic diversity is stunning; a comparative
study of human languages led to the techniques
and theories that became the foundation for
linguistic anthropology. Linguistic anthropologists
investigate everything from the sounds of
language to the rules that govern their
combinations and usage and their variations
in different styles and dialects. Early linguistic
anthropology sought to document and preserve
languages, but today it also looks at vernacular
speech forms, socialization, sign languages and
even gestures. Japanese, for example, is highly
context-dependent, often omitting the subject
entirely and employing a passive construction.
The language lends itself to uses that avoid
direct confrontation and rely instead on the
speaker's ability to subtly manipulate the tone
of certain words in ways that indicate the
relational status, gender, age and proximity of
speakers. Speaking Japanese requires more than
mastery of the grammatical rules; you also need
an appreciation of a cultural context in which
empathy and status markers have a fundamental
social function.

RELATED TOPICS
See also
LANGUAGE
page 82

SYMBOLS
page 84

3-SECOND ORIGIN
Linguistic anthropology
studies the structure and
use of language to discover
how culture and language
influence each other.

3-MINUTE DESCENT
'Semantics' refers to
the meaning of words,
and poses some tricky
problems when comparing
languages. Linguistic
anthropologists like Anna
Wierzbicka compared
dozens of languages and
found a small number of
'semantic primes' (simple
words that cannot
be defined by other
terms) constituting a
'metalanguage' of words
that exist across virtually
all languages. This
metalanguage allows us to
create precise translations
and comparisons between
cultural concepts using a
universally shared lexicon.

3-SECOND BIOGRAPHIES
DELL HYMES
1927–2009
American anthropologist who
used the terms 'communicative
competence' and 'speech
communities' to focus on the
use of language in relationships

ANNA WIERZBICKA
1938–
Polish linguist known for her
work in cross-cultural linguistics

30-SECOND TEXT
Jason Danely

*Linguistics helps us
understand how human
language has shaped
the way we think,
communicate and
interact with each other.*

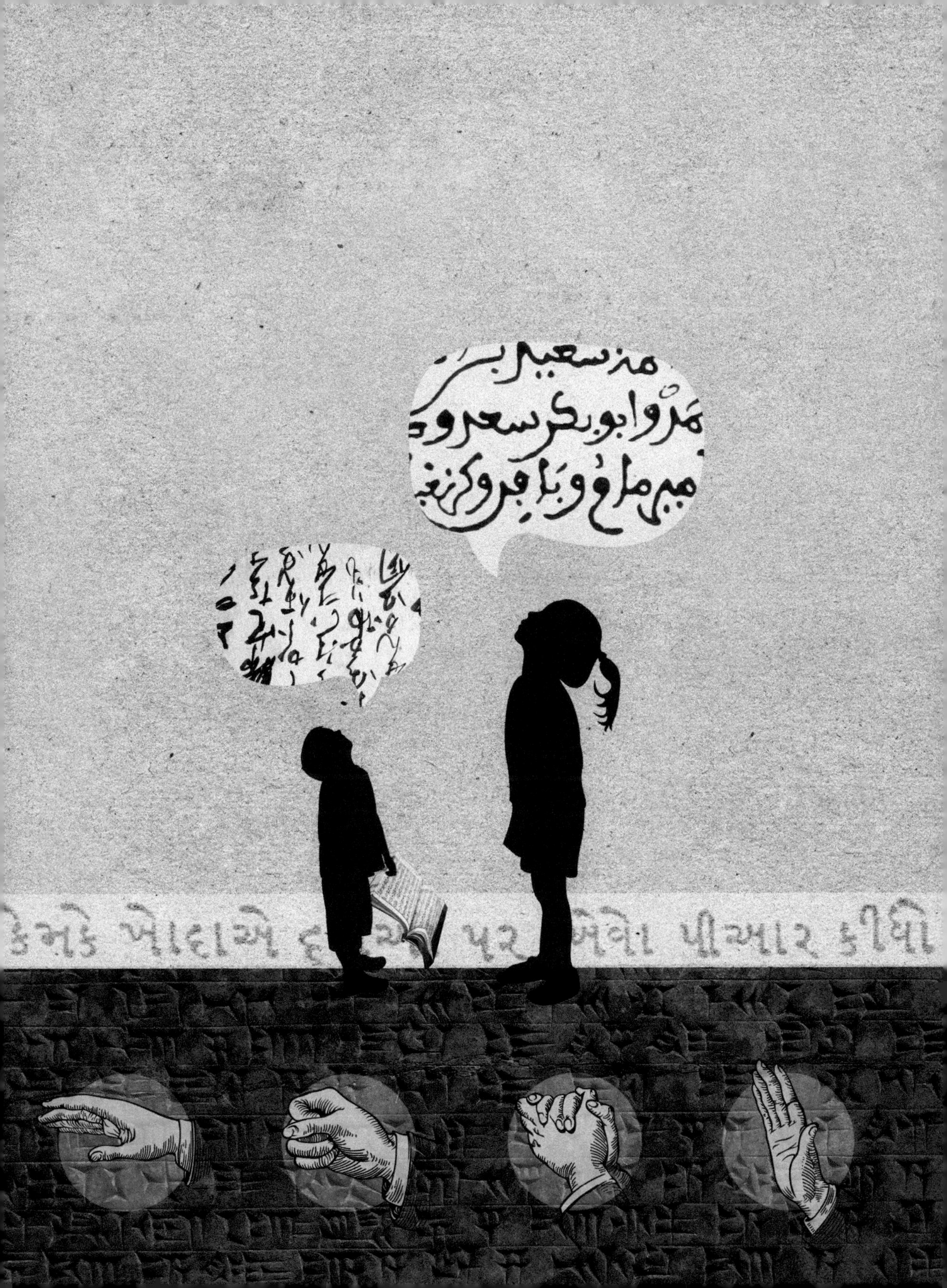

LANGUAGE

the 30-second anthropology

The ways we communicate our experience have been enhanced by the evolution of our vocal apparatus and our brains, which have a keen ability to discern what others are thinking. Since our language developed together with new capacities for social cooperation, we can hardly distinguish between the emergence of language and culture – some time during the Middle Palaeolithic. Both language and culture are learned systems of arbitrary symbols used together to encode knowledge of the world in a way that can be shared with others, and both are extremely adaptable. Today, there are more than 7,000 languages, many of which can be grouped, like people, into families with shared characteristics derived from a common heritage. At least 820 distinct languages (not merely dialects) are spoken by about 7 million inhabitants of Papua New Guinea, the highest density of any place on Earth. Most Papuans depend on the use of *tok pisin*, a language that has no native speakers, but acts as a common language between speech communities. A pidgin that develops into a native language is called a creole. As more people interact with speakers of different languages, many languages have become extinct while new mixed languages and unique speech communities are being born.

RELATED TOPICS
See also
LINGUISTICS
page 80

SYMBOLS
page 84

3-SECOND ORIGIN
Using language is uniquely human, and our primary way of learning and relating; its diversity reveals a process of adaptation still going on today.

3-MINUTE DESCENT
In traditional usage, Scottish people have at least 421 expressions for snow, including 'flindrikin' (a slight snow shower) and 'skelf' (a large snowflake). But do Scots perceive weather differently? The 'Sapir-Whorf Hypothesis', named after Edward Sapir and Benjamin Whorf, suggests that language affects how we think. A rich vocabulary not only helps us describe our world, but literally changes it into a form difficult for non-speakers to recognize.

3-SECOND BIOGRAPHIES
EDWARD SAPIR
1884–1939
American anthropologist who worked mostly with Native Americans (Omaha, Crow) and argued that words were not merely labels for a shared reality, but created different kinds of realities for speakers

BENJAMIN WHORF
1897–1941
American linguist who with his mentor Edward Sapir developed the principle of 'linguistic relativity'

30-SECOND TEXT
Jason Danely

Language is central to our understanding of the world; can we think without vocabulary to represent ideas, objects and experiences?

SYMBOLS
the 30-second anthropology

3-SECOND ORIGIN
To comprehend our insatiable desire to make sense of ourselves, our world and each other, look no further than the way we represent these things using symbols.

3-MINUTE DESCENT
The ecstatic worshippers at Kataragama, Sri Lanka, are known for fire-walking, piercing and other forms of extreme self-mortification. These acts, and the dramatically matted hair of the devotees that perform them, are both public symbols of faith and personal symbols or representations of an inner psychic turmoil. Symbols bridge these two worlds, giving a special place for the afflicted, as well as easing their pain.

French author Marcel Proust ate a madeleine (a small cake), and wrote a seven-volume novel. Of course the novel – *Remembrance of Things Past* – wasn't all about the madeleine, but rather the associations it evoked. The madeleine could not be understood outside of Proust's creation of his narrative – his art of crafting symbols into stories. Symbols are objects, images, sounds and representations that stand for something else within a given context. For anthropologists, the interpretation of symbols depends on paying attention to this context and the various associations that link it to the symbol. Some anthropologists, like Clifford Geertz, have been drawn to symbols' complexity and their transience – and, most of all, the way they help us create meaning. The potency of symbols is in their ability to condense a large number of meanings (even contradictory ones) and communicate them with an immediacy that we perceive, in part, unconsciously. Throughout history people have rallied behind symbols in war and in peace. An image of a cherry blossom may appear to be no more than a representation of a flower; but as a symbol it can represent life, death, youth, nation and home. To a Japanese kamikaze pilot in the Second World War, a symbol like that could have deadly power.

RELATED TOPICS
See also
RITUAL & CEREMONY
page 86

CLIFFORD GEERTZ
page 102

RELIGION & BELIEF
page 114

3-SECOND BIOGRAPHIES
CLIFFORD GEERTZ
1926–2006
American anthropologist who approached culture as a system of symbols and meanings that can be interpreted through ethnography

GANANATH OBEYESEKERE
1930–
Sri Lankan psychological anthropologist who connected the observable dimensions of symbols in public rituals to the way afflicted people represented their inner lives

30-SECOND TEXT
Jason Danely

The cherry blossom and the poppy evoke an intellectual and emotional response to those aware of their deep meanings.

RITUAL & CEREMONY

the 30-second anthropology

3-SECOND ORIGIN
Ritual and ceremony
abound in social life –
whether in a wedding,
funeral, coronation, formal
opening, prize giving,
religious ceremony or event
to mark the seasons.

3-MINUTE DESCENT
The rituals and ceremonies
that accompany us through
life may appear to be
historical and permanent,
but in fact are in a constant
state of flux and
reinvention. They may
move across cultural
boundaries, borrow
different elements from
each other and compete
with one another. In
western Europe the formal
state-ordained wedding
was unknown in the
medieval period, when a
simple spoken agreement
was made and witnessed
by family, friends and
neighbours.

French folklorist Arnold van Gennep emphasized the transitional power of rituals for those who participate in them – and coined the well-known phrase 'rites of passage'. For him, ritual represents a state of indeterminacy, and this gives rise to the possibility of change from one state of existence to another. Think of a graduation ceremony. At the beginning, students are regarded as graduands. But after the robed university vice-chancellor has laid his or her hands on them in front of the collected university, graduands become graduates – and enjoy a permanent change in their status. Emile Durkheim saw ritual acts as the way in which society inculcates social order through collective action. In this approach, the sensory experiences that are embodied in the ceremony – music, scent, visual appearance –help to render participants susceptible to the content of the ritual, which may be expressed symbolically, or explicitly through a liturgical or secular text or speech. Later another anthropologist, Edmund Leach, emphasized the way in which ritual often reflects or enacts a society's founding myth. In the United States, the pledge of allegiance so familiar to schoolchildren and recited by those taking citizenship is a ritualized retelling of the formation of the US and reflects the historical struggles of the founding fathers.

RELATED TOPICS
See also
RELIGION & BELIEF
page 114

IDENTITY
page 116

3-SECOND BIOGRAPHIES
EMILE DURKHEIM
1858–1917
French intellectual and founder
of sociology who emphasized
the importance of studying
collective social life and
institutions

ARNOLD VAN GENNEP
1873–1957
French folklorist and
ethnographer, chiefly known
today for his book *Les Rites
de Passage*

EDMUND LEACH
1910–89
British social anthropologist,
ethnographer of Myanmar and
Sri Lanka, who introduced
structuralism into Britain

30-SECOND TEXT
David Shankland

*Ceremonies and rituals
are used to mark the
stages of life, and the
passage of time, across
the world.*

DEATH

the 30-second anthropology

There is a world of difference

between dying and death. The purists will argue that we start to die before we are born and while this carries some truth, it is pedantic in the extreme. The process of dying probably scares us more than any other thing in life, because it leads to the great unknown event that is death – an event from which no one returns. For an organism, death is a singular event. Cells die every day without necessarily affecting the existence of the organism, but if tissues or organs cease to function and 'die', then – without medical intervention – the host will ultimately fail. The fact that an organism can technically die while its cells, organs and tissues can be kept alive artificially by a life-support machine is a modern phenomenon that reflects human ingenuity and our determination to defy the process of dying. Death is normally detected through the lack of three vital corporeal signs – a pulse from the heart, breath from the lungs and a signal from the brain. It is the separation of the physicality of death from the spiritual event that makes the subject one of intense fascination to us.

RELATED TOPICS
See also
RITUAL & CEREMONY
page 86

RELIGION & BELIEF
page 114

3-SECOND ORIGIN
Death is the final frontier – the inevitable experience that we must all face alone with no knowledge of what, if anything, lies beyond.

3-MINUTE DESCENT
Death is not just a physical and spiritual experience: it is also a social event and a lucrative commercial industry. The ritual that surrounds the event and the way in which we dispose of human remains are ingrained within the culture of different human communities. Nobody 'did' death with such outrageous solemnity, pomp and ceremony as the Victorians and often the event could be superbly resplendent for everyone – including the deceased.

3-SECOND BIOGRAPHY
QUEEN VICTORIA
1819–1901
A reigning widow who defined death as an art (ars moriendi) and mourning as a culture

30-SECOND TEXT
Sue Black

How we deal with death is about more than recording the physical signs of the body ceasing to function.

ART & ARTEFACT

the 30-second anthropology

Art and artefacts are the products of human creativity, ingenuity and skill. We keep and circulate them to tell a story about who we are and what we value. The most mundane of artefacts – a hair comb or a glass bead, say – can reveal not only a way of life but also a way of making meaning. And in creating works of art we extended this process from the practical to the imaginative, giving form to dreams and prejudices and creating stories about who we are or could be. The earliest examples of Palaeolithic art were lifelike copies of the natural world, but they were also full of strange and mysterious images that suggest a vivid capacity to express novel, abstract ideas. As social organization became more complex and artisans had more time and resources to develop their talents, art's storytelling became an ideological tool of powerful leaders and religious groups. From the Aztecs to the Romans, artistic images linked rulers and gods in a conquest of hearts and minds. Today, anthropologists see the dynamic interactions between art's emotional, ideological and economic power in new digital arts, as they spread globally, transforming into countless mashups, remixes and adaptations. Through all of this, art continues to tell stories about both the creative individual and the aesthetics of culture.

3-SECOND ORIGIN
From cave paintings to smartphones, we give form to the human story by creating art and artefacts.

3-MINUTE DESCENT
The colonial era from the sixteenth to the mid-twentieth century inspired a taste for exotic new art and antiquities. This prompted artisans to cater to the market, inventing a new 'traditional' form of characteristic art when there had been more diversity. Sometimes producing meaningful or sacred art for commercial sale is criticized. Australian Aboriginal artists, for example, can do a lucrative trade in colourful 'dreaming' paintings, but some believe these reveal too many secrets.

RELATED TOPICS
See also
CRAFT
page 66

SYMBOLS
page 84

3-SECOND BIOGRAPHIES
FRANZ BOAS
1858–1942
German-American anthropologist, one of the first to recognize the value of 'primitive art'

ALFRED GELL
1945–97
British social anthropologist who combined aesthetic and semiotic approaches with anthropology to develop theories about the social function of art as a 'technology of enchantment'

30-SECOND TEXT
Jason Danely

Reality and imagination meet in art, where humans create pieces based on both fantasy and the material world.

WHY DO WE CARE?

the 30-second anthropology

Each of us has received care and given care, but dig a bit deeper and we find just how complex this engagement is. Compared to non-human primates, humans exhibit a much more advanced propensity for 'mind reading' and 'perspective-taking' that makes us really interested in each other. This capacity for empathy didn't arise after we became 'civilized' modern humans. Archaeologists have found evidence that the sick and frail received care as early as 1.7 million years ago. They argue that had we relied only on brute force, we might not have developed the language skills or cooperative practices that were critical to our survival. It might not have been possible for humans to survive the long dependent infancy (longer than any other mammal) had we not first learned to take care of each other in ways that our ancestors did not. Today, the care of the young and old, sick and hungry can be observed in every human society, along with customs and traditions that reinforce compassion, love and connection. These pro-social emotions, deeply rooted in our human pasts, are the basis of gift exchange and adornment, kinship and affinity, religion and art.

3-SECOND ORIGIN
It is the ways we care, not the ways we quarrel, that make us uniquely human.

3-MINUTE DESCENT
American biological anthropologist Sarah Blaffer Hrdy observes that humans 'alloparent': they care for the offspring of their group regardless of maternity. That caring feeling we get when we see, hear or even smell babies might be attributed to the evolution of this alloparenting mechanism. Cross-cultural studies of childcare support Hrdy, showing that mothers and fathers are the least likely family members to care for small children in most places in the world.

RELATED TOPICS
See also
KINSHIP
page 124

PAUL FARMER
page 144

3-SECOND BIOGRAPHIES
ARTHUR KLEINMAN
1941–
American medical and psychological anthropologist whose personal experience of caring for his wife after her diagnosis with dementia led him to expand theories of care as fundamental, moral, existential and universal

SARAH BLAFFER HRDY
1946–
American biological anthropologist who uses insights from primatology and evolutionary psychology to look at the importance of women in human evolution

30-SECOND TEXT
Jason Danely

Human societies rely on members caring for each other.

MIGRATION

Berlin Wall Barrier built by the Communist East German Republic that cut off West Berlin from West Germany. Construction began on 13 August 1961 and the wall divided the city until political unrest in East Germany led to its 'opening' in November 1989, paving the way for eventual German reunification on 3 October 1990.

Bronze Age The Bronze Age is the period of human history that typically sees the use of bronze metal, early writing and increased urbanization. In the Middle East it dates from around 3300–1200 BCE and in Europe from 3200–600 BCE.

cultural anthropology The study of cultural variation in human groups that typically makes use of participant observation and extended field study.

cultural materialism Anthropological theory developed by Marvin Harris in the 1960s and 70s. Cultural materialists argue that human cultural variation can be explained via a materialist approach because societies develop through trial and error, suggesting that anything that is not useful would not persist.

game theory The use of mathematical models to explore how decisions are made based on the relative benefit or cost incurred by individuals or groups. Game theory is often illustrated by the 'Hawk-Dove Game', also known as 'Chicken', which pits two players against each other. The idea is that while both players are rewarded if one concedes, each player's best move is determined by the actions of the other.

humanism The idea that humans should use reason to improve the lives of all. It is often associated with atheism and has a strong science-based focus.

in-group and out-group Favouritism directed to members who belong to the same group. Perhaps the best known example is 'the old boys' network'. It is a mechanism that can operate both consciously and subconsciously in human groups.

indigenous A term used to describe the earliest inhabitants of a region and their living descendants.

Neanderthal An advanced species of hominin that lived in Europe and Asia between approximately 250,000 and 30,000 years ago. They developed many advanced behaviours and interbred with humans several times. The reason behind their extinction remains one of the most intriguing questions in human evolution.

Neolithic period Beginning in the Middle East around 10,000 years ago before spreading, it was the period that saw the development of farming and the use of secondary products from livestock such as skins, milk and other materials.

post-colonialism An umbrella term that covers research into the impact of the colonial and imperial policies of (generally) European powers on indigenous peoples up to the mid-twentieth century.

push and pull factors The large number of factors influencing human economic migration. Push factors are generally negative, such as not enough jobs, poor prospects or war, while pull factors are based on positive perceptions, such as better quality of life or plentiful jobs.

thick descriptions An explanation of human behaviour that also describes the context of the behaviour in order to make it accessible to those outside of that group.

NAVIGATION

the 30-second anthropology

Comprehending how people in prehistory understood space, their patterns of movement, their boat design and how they navigated in the absence of modern technology tells us a huge amount about them and their culture. By the first European contact with Polynesian islanders in the Pacific in the 1500s, virtually every Polynesian island was inhabited. Dutch explorers wrote of sailboats in Tonga, while more than 3,000 km (2,000 miles) away Captain James Cook encountered hundreds of sailing boats in Tahiti and Hawaii. French explorers, impressed upon seeing people's seafaring skills, named present-day Samoa the 'Navigator Islands'. We know that Polynesian seafarers used 'dead-reckoning' – knowing where you are starting from and judging your progress on the basis of your direction and the amount of time you've been at sea; following rising or setting stars; or using 'wind compasses' that charted predictable wind patterns. Recent ethnographic investigation and genetic analyses demonstrate that, despite some islands being nearly 10,000 km (6,000 miles) apart, the Polynesian islanders share a common heritage, indicating that they navigated purposefully and likely reached the Americas long before the Europeans did.

RELATED TOPICS

See also
BRONISLAW MALINOWSKI
page 78

TRADE
page 100

BORDERS
page 104

3-SECOND BIOGRAPHIES

FERDINAND MAGELLAN
1480–1521
Portuguese explorer, sailor and navigator who took part in the first circumnavigation of the globe in 1519–22

THOR HEYERDAHL
1914–2002
Norwegian explorer and ethnographer known for his *Kon-Tiki* expedition, which in 1947 sailed from South America to the Tuamotu Islands (French Polynesia) to demonstrate that ancient people could have made long sea voyages

30-SECOND TEXT
Djuke Veldhuis

Where our ancestors interpreted the landscape to find their way, we simply follow instructions on sat-nav.

3-SECOND ORIGIN

Navigation is the science of getting your feet, ship, land-vehicle or spacecraft from place to place – and typically requires you to determine a position, course and distance travelled.

3-MINUTE DESCENT

The Lapita people, ancestors of the Polynesians and modern-day Pacific Islanders, first sailed from coastal New Guinea about 5,000 years ago. They reached the Solomon Islands about 3,000 years ago and gradually expanded east. Their navigators crossed thousands of kilometres of open ocean using their sense and knowledge of stars and swells, ocean and sky passed on through oral tradition in boats made entirely from natural materials without maps or sextants.

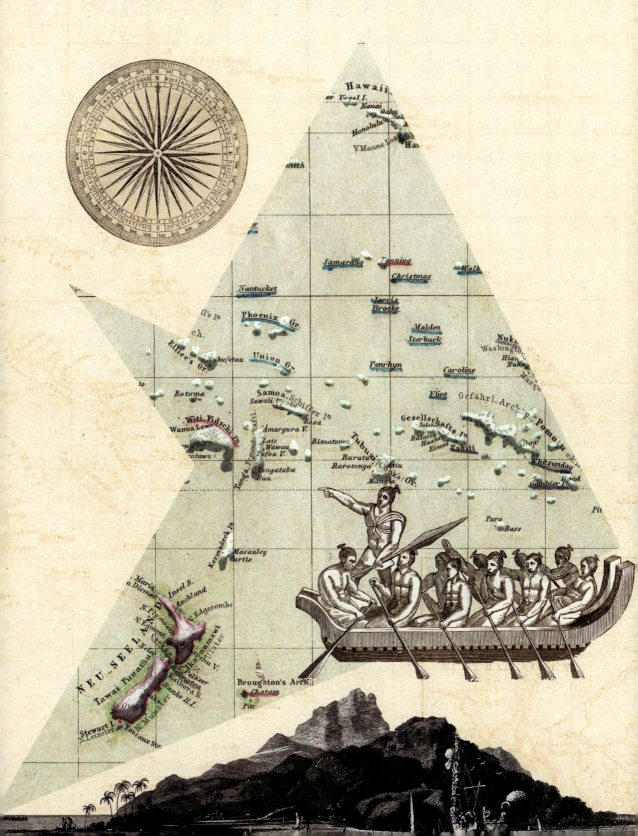

TRADE

the 30-second anthropology

The earliest evidence for trade

– exchange between two or more geographically distinct locations – comes from the Neolithic period. By the end of the Bronze Age, complex networks of inter-regional trade had developed. These were expanded and elaborated in later centuries. The development of sea travel was important in extending the range of trading activities. For archaeologists, the maritime aspect of trade offers an opportunity to study whole cargoes found in shipwrecks and, for this reason, the development of underwater archaeology has been important in studying ancient trade, especially in the Mediterranean region. Roman trading systems brought goods and people from across the Empire to northwest Europe, and played an important part in the origins of European urbanism, as in London. When the Western Roman Empire collapsed, this trading system was replaced in the seventh century CE by one focused on the North Sea. From the eighth century on this was further developed. During the Viking period urban trading centres emerged across Scandinavia and along the river-systems of Eastern Europe, linking these areas to wider trading networks. The resulting European trading system laid the foundation of the medieval trading networks that form the basis of those of today.

3-SECOND ORIGIN
The international trading system central to the twenty-first-century world economy originated largely in first millennium CE Europe and was later globalized by imperial expansion.

3-MINUTE DESCENT
Trade is often associated with using money to buy and sell material things. However, archaeology and history show that trading systems existed prior to any form of money, and trade often involves non-material goods, as in today's financial sector. All trade also takes place within moral and cultural frameworks, often ultimately derived from religious beliefs and values. This is very clearly seen in the abolition of the post-medieval European slave trade.

RELATED TOPICS
See also
SETTLEMENT
page 76

NAVIGATION
page 98

GLOBALIZATION
page 148

3-SECOND BIOGRAPHIES
SIR JAMES LANCASTER
c. 1554–1618
English commander of the first commercial voyage of the newly formed East India Company, which over the next 250 years would grow to become the first truly global business

SIR MOSES I. FINLEY
1912–86
American-born classical scholar whose book *The Ancient Economy* developed new ways of thinking about trade and exchange in the past

30-SECOND TEXT
Ken Dark

Trade has a physical and cultural impact on societies, exchanging ideas along with goods.

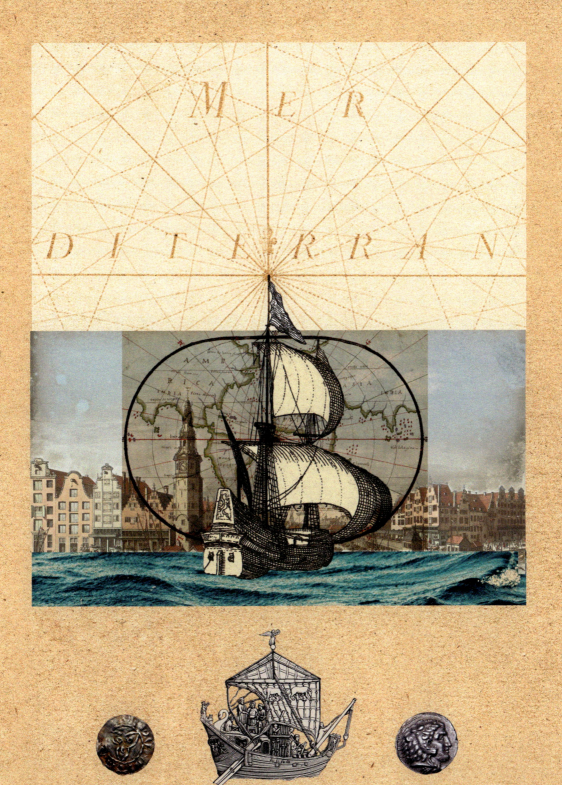

23 August 1926
Born in San Francisco

1943
Volunteers for the U.S. Navy, serving for two years

1946
Attends Antioch College on the G.I. Bill

1956
Graduates with a PhD in anthropology from the Harvard University Department of Social Relations

1960–70
Professor of anthropology at the University of Chicago

1970
Becomes professor of social science at the Institute for Advanced Study in Princeton

1973
Publishes his essay 'Deep Play: Notes on the Balinese Cockfight' and the collection *The Interpretation of Cultures*, which begins with an essay on thick description

1987
Marries second wife, Karen Blu, with whom he stays until his death

1988
Publishes *Works and Lives: The Anthropologist as Author*. This unique book looks at the literary styles of four major anthropologists

2000
Retires as professor emeritus from the Institute of Advanced Studies, Princeton

30 October 2006
Dies in Philadelphia, Pennsylvania, as a result of complications after heart surgery

CLIFFORD GEERTZ

Born in San Francisco in 1926, Clifford Geertz served in the U.S. Navy during the Second World War and then attended Antioch College in Yellow Springs, Ohio. He studied to become a writer, but changed to philosophy. He took a PhD in anthropology at Harvard University and then became a professor of anthropology at the University of Chicago.

Early in his career he investigated cultures in Indonesia, then from the mid-1960s onward switched his primary focus to Morocco. From 1970 to 2000 he was professor of social science at the Institute for Advanced Study in Princeton.

One of the most famous ethnographic fieldwork episodes starred Geertz, his wife, the police and a few fighting cocks. Geertz and his wife were watching an illegal cockfight in Bali when the police arrived and sent the crowd running. Instinctively, the anthropologists ran as well, ending up sitting at a stranger's house just as the police arrived. Thanks to the quick thinking of the locals, Geertz and his wife fooled the police, and relations in the village were never the same again.

This account, given in his 1973 essay 'Deep Play: Notes on the Balinese Cockfight', is more than just a humorous anecdote from the field. Geertz was making a case for a new dynamic narrative style that privileged specific local events as they happened over the symmetry of ideal structures. He modelled culture as a collection of texts that 'the anthropologist strains to read over the shoulders of those to whom they properly belong'.

In his descriptions of religion, ritual and culture in Morocco and Indonesia, Geertz found cultures that were complex, full of spontaneous disruptions and uncertain outcomes. Despite this, however, people found ways to get along because they shared stories, symbols and values. Geertz argued that anthropologists should develop 'thick descriptions' of culture (descriptions that explain behaviour in context).

Geertz was a captivating storyteller – and his approach to culture revived a humanistic and aesthetic sensibility that stood in sharp contrast to the scientific approaches of cultural materialists. This struck a chord with scholars in the post-Vietnam, post-colonial era, who saw an urgent need to question existing political orders and assumptions.

This could be done, in part, by foregrounding the narratives of marginalized or oppressed people and interpreting these thick descriptions within critical frameworks. This shift in the agenda of cultural anthropology owes much of its inspiration to Geertz. For Geertz, cultural anthropology was 'not an experimental science in search of law, but an interpretive one in search of meaning'.

Jason Danely

BORDERS

the 30-second anthropology

The fixed borders we associate with countries have their origin in the territories of the animal kingdom, where territorial behaviour can be essential for survival and reproduction. Two things are important: competition and the ability to defend resources in an area. Successful defence allows you to gain access to food, mates and shelter. Time spent staking out a territory, through scent-marking (tigers, ungulates), vocalizations (wolves, monkeys), posturing (cichlid fish), physical patrols (chimpanzees) or a combination of these demands time and energy that could be spent on other things. An optimal balance needs to be struck, depending on the quality of your territory. This is as true for humans as it is for other species. For example, some birds, such as swifts, do not need to defend territories because the insects they hunt are plentiful and unpredictably distributed. One way for humans to secure territory is to build physical barriers. Since 1950 the number of border fences has risen dramatically. It slowed temporarily with the fall of the Berlin Wall in 1989 as globalization swept in. However, in the early twenty-first century, nations sought to control smuggling, terrorism and influxes in migrants and refugees, leading to a rise from some 15 barriers in 2000 to around 70 in 2016.

RELATED TOPICS
See also
SETTLEMENT
page 76

SYMBOLS
page 84

WAR & AGGRESSION
page 136

3-SECOND ORIGIN
Borders are invisible lines, defined by social consensus or force, which form geographic boundaries separating human groups, countries, political entities or internal administrative districts from one another.

3-MINUTE DESCENT
Formal borders provide a foundation for cultural, political and economic structures, but they are essentially arbitrary and imagined communities. Why then are individuals willing to fight for 'their' country? Psychologically we relate easily to categories (friend/enemy; self/other; civilized/ uncivilized). These concepts have strong symbolic significance; borders are a physical manifestation of socially constructed categories that allow people to form their sense of identity and belonging.

3-SECOND BIOGRAPHIES
JOHN MAYNARD SMITH
1920–2004
British evolutionary biologist and geneticist known for applying game theory to evolution; this also served as a model for examining territorial interactions (for example, the Hawk-Dove Game)

KENICHI OHMEA
1943–
Japanese organizational theorist and author of *The Borderless World* (1990), which argues that national borders are less relevant than ever before and discusses the road to globalization

30-SECOND TEXT
Djuke Veldhuis

Physical barriers to enforce control of movement have been used at some borders.

ECONOMIC MIGRANTS

the 30-second anthropology

3-SECOND ORIGIN
Economic migration drives our economies, but places pressure on cities – with more than 243 million people moving between states and more than 740 million relocating internally.

3-MINUTE DESCENT
While many relocate for economic reasons, the dividing line between economic migration and other types of migration is not clear-cut. Refugees fleeing persecution or migrants hoping to join family abroad may also wish to improve their economic fortunes. The United States was populated by people with mixed motivations. As noted in Emma Lazarus's poem for the Statue of Liberty, migrants include the 'tired', 'poor' and 'huddled masses yearning to breathe free'.

Economic migration occurs both between and within states. The United Nations estimates that in 2015 there were more than 243 million international migrants, the bulk of whom moved from less to more economically developed regions. In addition, there are estimated to be more than 740 million internal migrants, with a great deal of movement occurring within China and India. While the causes of outflows are often interconnected, economic migration is characterized in terms of push and pull factors, the dominant view being that migrants move to improve their wage earnings. The pressure to absorb economic migrants is increasingly felt in cities, especially the more than 36 megacities – cities with populations over 10 million, the largest being Tokyo and Shanghai. In terms of immigration, economic migrants are defined by their skills set, which determines their possibilities for entry and settlement. Highly skilled migrants, including professionals, enjoy greater access to competitive markets like the United States, though all countries engage low-skilled and often unregulated labour to sustain agriculture, construction and other industries. The European Union is unique in permitting the free movement of EU nationals, which grants them the right to search for and do work in another EU state.

RELATED TOPICS
See also
BORDERS
page 104

REFUGEES
page 108

GLOBALIZATION
page 148

3-SECOND BIOGRAPHY
EMMA LAZARUS
1849–87
American poet, best known for her sonnet 'The New Colossus', which was inscribed after her death at the foot of the Statue of Liberty in New York: it calls the statue 'Mother of Exiles'

30-SECOND TEXT
Brad K. Blitz

The inscription on the Statue of Liberty is a paean to the benefits brought by economic migrants and the power of humans seeking a better way of life.

REFUGEES
the 30-second anthropology

The idea of refugees – people fleeing their country to escape persecution or fighting – is recent in human history, for it has meaning only when there are borders, nations and states. The challenge for both refugee and host community is the human tendency to categorize people as 'in-group' or 'out-group'. People tend to favour family (in-group), while having more neutral or sceptical attitudes towards non-kin or outsiders (out-group). This is by no means universal, and when resources are plentiful individuals from different groups may peacefully coexist. But, as the local environment changes (for example, food supply goes up or down) so does behaviour. Attitudes towards refugees vary according to political stability, wealth, employment rates and existing population diversity. The meaning and value humans give to cultural systems of behaviour and norms, notably religion and ethnicity, in combination with wealth inequalities and territorial behaviour over resources (oil, water, food) lies at the root of many refugee crises. Geography plays a significant role, too: in 2015, 86 per cent of refugees sought safety in low- and middle-income countries close to the situations of conflict.

3-SECOND ORIGIN
Refugees are defined as people in flight from conflict or persecution; they are protected under international law, and must not be returned where their lives and freedom are at risk.

3-MINUTE DESCENT
Were Neanderthals Europe's first 'refugees'? They faced a dual threat: climate change and competition from modern humans who arrived from Africa 45,000 years ago. The last Neanderthals survived in southern *refugia*, small areas of relatively livable conditions, on the Iberian Peninsula. Unfortunately, by their very nature *refugia* tend to isolate populations and split Neanderthal populations into small groups that were not viable – leading to their extinction some time after 40,000 years ago.

RELATED TOPICS
See also
BORDERS
page 104

ECONOMIC MIGRANTS
page 106

3-SECOND BIOGRAPHIES
AFGHAN REFUGEES
After the Soviet Union occupied Afghanistan in 1979, 5 million fled; since 1990 the number of refugees has not fallen below 2 million per year

SYRIAN REFUGEES
From 2011–16 an estimated 11 million fled their homes, with around 6.6 million displaced inside the country; 4.8 million were in Turkey, Jordan, Iraq and Egypt, and 1 million requested asylum in Europe, particularly Germany and Sweden

30-SECOND TEXT
Djuke Veldhuis

The plight of refugees can provoke compassion and hostility in equal measure.

IDEAS

affinity A term used in social anthropology to describe the relationship between people created by marriage. As well as the married couple, it can also be used to describe an extended network between families and larger social networks.

anti-Semitism A form of racism directed specifically against Jewish peoples.

biometrics Human measurements, such as fingerprints, iris pattern, DNA and facial features, used to establish identity in everything from crime detection to passports and computer security.

consanguinity Literally meaning blood relation, this is used to describe the degrees of relatedness between members of a family lineage back to a common or shared ancestor. Consanguinity is a legal basis used to rule in disputes over inheritance and in religious law for rulings over cousin marriage.

cultural anthropology The study of cultural variation in human groups that typically makes use of participant observation and extended field study.

DNA Deoxyribonucleic acid is a chain-like structure found in the chromosomes of almost every living thing apart from a handful of viruses. As the primary genetic material of an organism it controls the production of proteins and transmits inherited traits, acting as the blueprint for development.

ethnography (ethnographic research) The systematic social-cultural study of people; the term is used more generally to refer to the written account of such research.

fieldwork A term used across anthropology to refer to data collection. Fieldwork can range from long-term archaeological excavation of a hominin fossil-bearing site to participant observation of social-cultural practices in one's own local community.

forebrain The frontal portion of the brain. In *Homo sapiens* the change in shape of the frontal bone of the skull suggests that the forebrain altered shape relative to other hominin species.

indigenous A term used to describe the earliest inhabitants of a region and their living descendants.

interpretive drift A gradual and often imperceptible shift in how one interprets an activity as one becomes more deeply embedded in that activity.

neocortex Area of the brain located in the cerebral cortex that influences sight and hearing. In mammal species, it is generally considered to be the most recently developed region of the brain. Primates, especially humans, have large neocortex areas and they are closely associated with managing social relationships.

neoliberalism Updated interpretation of the economic ideas developed by Adam Smith in *The Wealth of Nations*. It gained traction after the collapse of the Soviet Union and focuses on the responsibility of the individual over the nation state.

postmodernism Less a theory and more a way of thinking about the anthropological world. It developed in the US and France in the 1970s and argues that everything that we know about the world is our own construction based on our experiences and prejudices and must be deconstructed through anthropological discourse.

psychological anthropology Interdisciplinary branch of anthropology that explores the relationship between mental processes and cultural practice.

social anthropology Branch of anthropology that studies human societies and culture.

structural functionalism (also known as functionalism) A social anthropological theory that suggests that society is a complex system made up of mutually supportive elements that contribute to societal stability.

structuralism Based on the thinking of the social anthropologist Claude Lévi-Strauss, structuralism argues that there are shared structures in all societies that can be found across human cultural practice regardless of location in the world.

symbolic anthropology The study of the cultural use of symbols in human society and how the symbols used by a particular group can contribute to understanding them.

Zen Buddhism Japanese derivation of Mahayana Buddhism that focuses on the importance of meditation.

RELIGION & BELIEF

the 30-second anthropology

3-SECOND ORIGIN
Neither irrational superstition nor mere rationalization of the unknowable, religious belief makes the self, the senses and the social knowable, memorable and meaningful.

3-MINUTE DESCENT
Psychological anthropologist Tanya Luhrmann described how ordinary people come to believe in things that seem to contradict reality. She identified a slow process of adapting beliefs to one's own scepticism, called 'interpretive drift'. In this way, ordinary feelings, sensory experiences and life events are imaginatively interpreted in a religious framework. Through interpretive drift, doubt and commitment can work together to form religious beliefs.

Religion is one of the most aesthetically captivating and intellectually fascinating aspects of human culture – whether you spend a night dancing with ecstatic trance mediums or a day in silent meditation at a Zen monastery. Defining 'religion' is not a simple task, but most anthropologists agree that religions express collective realities related to the supernatural world. They can do so using ceremonies and rituals, such as festivals and feasts, which symbolically and emotionally absorb the individual into the world of their group and create a relational bridge to the divine. It is this collective nature of religion that sets it apart from idiosyncratic personal experiences and from other ways of engaging with the supernatural world, such as sorcery or witchcraft. Religious identity is often woven into the customs of everyday life, from clothes to food. Some religious practices seem bizarre and extreme to outsiders. Why would someone believe that gods speak to them in dreams or through them in possession? But people do have these experiences all the time, and attaching them to ideas about superhuman agency and religious meanings allows a suspension of disbelief and new possibilities for belonging and self-transformation. Religion, like art, brings imagination into the social sphere.

RELATED TOPICS
See also
SYMBOLS
page 84

RITUAL & CEREMONY
page 86

IDENTITY
page 116

3-SECOND BIOGRAPHIES
EMILE DURKHEIM
1858–1917
French sociologist who synthesized ethnographic accounts to suggest the primacy of collective rituals in the social evolution of religious life

TALAL ASAD
1932–
Saudi anthropologist who critically examines the effect of modernity on religious life

30-SECOND TEXT
Jason Danely

Culture, ascetics and personal experience meet and interact in the melting pot of human religious beliefs.

IDENTITY

the 30-second anthropology

Identity comes from Latin *idem* meaning 'the same' and gives rise to the word 'identical'. The ancient Greek philosopher Aristotle provided a simple law of identity A=A, which did not permit change. His fellow-philosopher Heraclitus recognized that in nature few things are identical and he modified the equation to A=A*, with the asterisk an indicator of change. To establish identity requires investigators to consider how much change they are prepared to tolerate before they can no longer confirm with confidence that something is identical. Change is one of the defining characteristics of the human being. Each person has many identities – physical, cultural, spiritual, professional and so on – and these do not necessarily remain static but can change quite dramatically over time. Establishing the identity of an individual requires an understanding of the inadequacies inherent in the measures we use to establish, compare and confirm it, while recognizing and managing the inevitability of change. Identity is a high-value commodity on the black market and identity theft is the fastest rising crime in our digital world – such that markers of our physical identity (biometrics) are being incorporated into everyday technology, for example fingerprints or face recognition to access mobile phones or computers.

RELATED TOPICS
See also
RACE
page 34

KINSHIP
page 124

GENDER
page 128

3-SECOND ORIGIN
Identity reaffirms that we are who we say we are, and that who we say we are is who we have always been.

3-MINUTE DESCENT
It is difficult to tell identical twins apart by looking at their facial appearance or mannerisms, but they are not identical. While they share the vast majority of their DNA, a number of anatomical details will differ and allow them to be separated with the same level of confidence as any two siblings of the same sex. Their fingerprints will be different as will their iris patterns and their superficial vein patterns.

3-SECOND BIOGRAPHY
ALPHONSE BERTILLON
1853–1914
French police officer who developed an identification system that became known as Bertillonage, the early forerunner of biometrics

30-SECOND TEXT
Sue Black

'Identity' refers both to our legal and physical personhood, as well as our complex and shifting perception of ourselves.

POLITICS

the 30-second anthropology

Fish are built to navigate the sea and birds the air. In the same way humans are built to navigate the conflicts of interest that arise naturally among members of a social species. In the Greek philosopher Aristotle's words, we are a *Zoon Politikon*, 'a political animal'. Politics is the art of getting what we want and our rich political tool kit includes everything from arguing over alliance-building to violence. While we often think of politics as the business of professional politicians, everyone constantly uses political tactics to get their way: when negotiating who should do the dishes, when discussing the placement of a playground in the local neighbourhood or when trying to secure that promotion at work. Politics is also an ancient activity. As a species, we have engaged in politics since our ancestors began living in social groups and needed to decide how to share meat, mates and prestige. Because of the ancestral nature of our political brain, we cannot always trust the political intuitions of ourselves or others. Research shows that our intuitions often reflect the solutions that worked within the small-scale groups of our ancestors rather than within the large-scale market societies of today.

Political machinations are not unique to humans. Chimpanzee behaviour suggests they can argue, lie and manipulate just as well as we can.

28 November 1908
Born to French Jewish parents

1931
After studying at the Sorbonne, qualifies as a teacher of philosophy

1935
Departs for Latin America as a visiting professor at São Paulo University and conducts fieldwork

1939
Returns to France

1940
Stripped of citizenship under anti-Jewish legislation and leaves France

1941
Arrives in the United States and spends the Second World War mainly in New York City, where he gets to know Roman Jakobson and Franz Boas

1948
Returns to Paris

1949
Publishes *The Elementary Structures of Kinship*

1959
Awarded chair in social anthropology at the Collège de France

1962
Publishes *La pensée sauvage* ('The Savage Mind')

1971
Publishes *Mythologiques*

1973
Elected to the Académie Française

30 October 2009
Dies in Paris, aged 100

CLAUDE LÉVI-STRAUSS

Claude Lévi-Strauss is known as the founder of structuralism, perhaps the most influential anthropological theory of all time.

He was born to French Jewish parents, and went to school in Paris. He studied philosophy at the Sorbonne, then became a schoolteacher. Already interested in anthropology, in 1935 he took up a role as a visiting university professor in Brazil, where he conducted fieldwork among the indigenous Indian population. This helped to spark an interest in mythology, which he explored for the rest of his life.

At the outbreak of the Second World War in 1939, he returned to France but was forced to leave by the anti-Semitic legislation of the French Vichy government, which stripped him of his citizenship and placed his life in danger. He travelled by boat to Martinique, and then eventually to New York, where he became one of the founders of the 'New School for Social Research'. There he was part of a circle of French intellectuals in exile, which included linguists such as Roman Jakobson, and he also became acquainted with Franz Boas, who famously died in his arms in a restaurant after suffering a heart attack.

On his return from New York, he submitted as part of his doctoral work *The Elementary Structures of Kinship* – which, when published, set a new direction in kinship studies by emphasizing alliance and exchange of brides between groups, rather than descent within lineages, which had previously been stressed in Anglo-Saxon anthropology.

He subsequently broadened this approach, asserting that what he was interested in was not empirical reality, but in the generating structures that underlie that reality. He demonstrated this form of structural approach in a series of volumes known as *Mythologiques*, which were devoted to the comparative analysis of a myth and its variations which he had encountered during his fieldwork.

This and many others of his works were translated into English and helped to shape the revolutionary intellectual currents of postmodernism, which came to dominate literary and artistic critical theory in the second half of the twentieth century. Within anthropology he quickly became popular and structural studies of myth began to abound. But his star appeared to wane as quickly as it rose, and today he is less read than he used to be. Yet, however easy it is to dismiss his sometimes extravagant claims, he is of more than historical importance, because it is difficult to refute his contention that the human mind both constrains and patterns culture.

David Shankland

HIERARCHY & LEADERSHIP

the 30-second anthropology

3-SECOND ORIGIN
All human societies have an idea of social order, but the way that this is achieved and imagined varies greatly.

3-MINUTE DESCENT
Anthropologists have developed various theories as to why people structure society as they do. Functionalism argued that social institutions derive from people's biological needs; structural functionalism said that culture reflects and perpetuates hierarchical social systems that lie behind it; structuralism emphasized that oppositional categories (such as life and death or up and down) common to all peoples have effects on our behaviour, culture and social structures.

The variety of ways in which societies order their affairs are an intriguing object of study for anthropologists – from the intricate caste systems of India to the peaceful hunter-gatherers of the Indonesian rainforest (who nevertheless possess a highly complex and graded spiritual cosmology); from the tribes of northern Africa, the peasant communities of Eurasia and the African precolonial kingdoms to the vast modern bureaucratic nation-states that today appear to be becoming ever more dominant. In peasant communities, the household is often the key social unit. In tribes, the wider patrilineage – descent (imagined or real) in the male line – may assume a more important role. In some small-scale hunter-gatherer societies, such as those in Indonesia, there may appear to be a strong egalitarian ethos, with no obvious leader. Anthropologists have long explored the way kinship plays a role in determining where and how a person fits into a social hierarchy. Clifford Geertz studied the way that symbol, charisma and myth interact with and sustain leadership. French scholar Pierre Bourdieu showed that hierarchies in modern nation-states tend to be dependent upon a complex interaction of rank, wealth, descent, attainment and culture.

RELATED TOPICS
See also
BRONISLAW MALINOWSKI
page 78

GENDER
page 128

GLOBALIZATION
page 148

3-SECOND BIOGRAPHIES
CLIFFORD GEERTZ
1926–2006
American pioneer of symbolic anthropology, the study of cultural symbols and how they can be used to interpret societies

PIERRE BOURDIEU
1930–2002
French anthropologist, specialist in North Africa and theorist of contemporary society

30-SECOND TEXT
David Shankland

How society is ordered, and where we stand in it, has been a concern since humans developed social groups.

KINSHIP

the 30-second anthropology

Kinship describes the way

individuals are organized into groups, roles and categories. It can be seen as one of the building blocks of human society. Anthropologists use kinship to understand social interaction, attitudes and motivations across societies. Age and gender also play important roles and the relative strength and importance of the bonds between kin vary across societies. The vocabulary of kinship includes terms that define our relation to others: mother, uncle, cousin and so on. The specific words used underline social norms and values. In England the term 'uncle' refers to the brothers of your mother or father. But if you are using Dani, which is spoken by people in Western New Guinea, 'uncle' refers only to your mother's brother; your father's brother is called your 'father'. Like language, kinship concepts are fluid and may change alongside cultural norms. In many modern industrialized economies the nuclear family (parents and children) forms a core unit. Here kinship ties exist at two levels: mother and father through marriage ('affinity') and each parent and child by blood relations through descent ('consanguinity'). In some countries co-habiting, same-sex couples who adopt children are legally recognized as a family unit even though there is no consanguinity.

3-SECOND ORIGIN
Kinship, alongside gender and age, is one of the key organizing principles of human society and serves as a basis for forming social groups and classifying people.

3-MINUTE DESCENT
'Blood runs thicker than water' goes the proverb. It implies that family relationships are more important than friends. In biology kinship refers to the degree of genetic relatedness between individual members of a species. Kin selection theory describes a strategy that favours the success of an individual's relatives even when it is at the expense of the individual. It has been used to explain behaviours such as altruism.

RELATED TOPICS
See also
WHY DO WE CARE?
page 92

CLAUDE LÉVI-STRAUSS
page 120

3-SECOND BIOGRAPHIES
LEWIS HENRY MORGAN
1818–81
American anthropologist best known for his work on kinship and social structure

ALFRED RADCLIFFE BROWN
1881–1955
English social anthropologist who did fieldwork in the Andaman Islands and across Polynesia and created a theory on social structures

DAVID MURRAY SCHNEIDER
1918–95
American cultural anthropologist who argued that kinship is a cultural system that varies among peoples

30-SECOND TEXT
Djuke Veldhuis

Family groups and the bonds they create help shape our societies.

DUNBAR'S NUMBER

the 30-second anthropology

Why do primates have such large brains compared to other mammals? This was the problem anthropologist Robin Dunbar set out to solve, examining the various competing explanations. The cognitive challenges posed by the environment were one; another theory (the 'social brain hypothesis') argued that primates have large brains because they live in socially complex societies: the larger the group, the bigger the brain. The neocortex in the forebrain is particularly important in processing social information. Dunbar went on to test the competing theories. Plotting the relationship between neocortex size and environmental complexity, he saw no obvious patterns. But on doing the same using primate group size – a proxy for social complexity – he found a highly significant result. Dunbar realized he could use a ratio of neocortical volume to total brain volume to predict average group size across species. He found that the average number of people with whom a person can maintain meaningful social relationships is around 150. In reality, this number is a range: social butterflies may have up to 200 acquaintances and over time the friends you have change. His conclusion is supported by anthropological studies and also extends to armies and organizations. Groups larger than 150 tend to be broken down into smaller subunits.

3-SECOND BIOGRAPHY
ROBIN DUNBAR
1947–
British anthropologist and primate behaviour specialist who focused on brain evolution and sociality in primates and developed 'Dunbar's number'

30-SECOND TEXT
Djuke Veldhuis

Dunbar's number provides a useful tool to look at how humans organize themselves into groups and interact with each other.

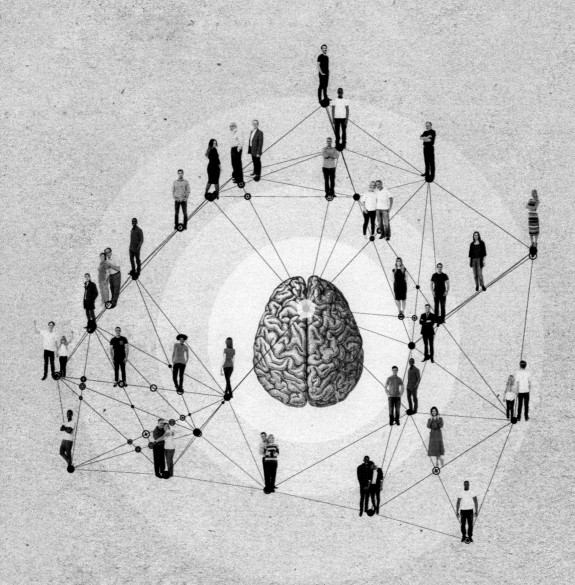

GENDER

the 30-second anthropology

Gender – the idea that men and women are different – affects us all and can play a fundamental role in how societies are organized. Gender is distinct from, and contrasts with, biological sex. Early women anthropologists such as Margaret Mead, Ruth Benedict and Phyllis Karberry were clearly aware of the importance of gender, but anthropologists only really began to focus on the topic in the 1970s. Some argued that ethnographic research, often unwittingly, featured men; while men inhabited an accessible 'public' sphere, women tended to be more in the 'private' sphere of the household. Anthropologists saw that gender hierarchy is established through multiple, mutually reinforcing constraints on women's behaviour that may encompass space, language, ritual, religion, property, knowledge and wealth. For example, in some societies women may be less free to move around than men or aspects of ritual may be closed to them; sometimes religion contains a core myth in which women are regarded as being dangerous to men. In some groups women are not given equal access to property or wealth. The accumulation of these different cultural factors leads to systematic inequality, which is very difficult to overcome.

RELATED TOPICS
See also
MARGARET MEAD
page 40

3-SECOND ORIGIN
Anthropologists today generally see gender as being socially constructed – the roles that the sexes fulfil are open to research and questioning.

3-MINUTE DESCENT
Gender is an area in which anthropology has made a fundamental contribution to modern social thought and policy. Anthropological approaches to gender have moved into mainstream research, often as part of wider debates about global inequality, the assumptions and ideas underlying Western science and neoliberalism. Investigations by anthropologists have clarified the diverse way that gender can be experienced across the world's communities in a globalized world.

3-SECOND BIOGRAPHIES
RUTH BENEDICT
1887–1948
American cultural anthropologist, author of *Patterns of Culture* (1934)

PHYLLIS KARBERRY
1910–77
Early field researcher on women, particularly in Aboriginal Australia

30-SECOND TEXT
David Shankland

Although traditionally viewed as a dichotomy, gender is a complex phenomenon in which individuals do not always correspond to normative gender roles.

MODERN PEOPLES

biodiversity The variety of organisms found in a particular habitat.

C-3PO Probably the most famous robot in cinema. In the *Star Wars* films, C-3PO acts not only as a translator between alien species but also as an interface between the human and computer worlds.

cystic fibrosis A genetic disease for which there is no known cure that primarily affects the lungs, causing breathing problems. It is an inherited autosomal recessive disease, which means that two copies of the cystic fibrosis mutation are present in sufferers. Carriers, those with a single copy, are asymptomatic.

DNA Deoxyribonucleic acid is a chain-like structure found in the chromosomes of almost every living thing apart from a handful of viruses. As the primary genetic material of an organism it controls the production of proteins and transmits inherited traits, acting as the blueprint for development.

Dolly the sheep Born on 5 July 1996, Dolly was the first cloned mammal from an adult cell. The process was carried out by scientists at the University of Edinburgh.

drug-resistant TB The common name for strains of tuberculosis which are immune to 'last line of defence' antibiotics. Drug-resistant TB is a perfect example of evolution in action and has been observed in TB strains since the first widespread use of antibiotics in the 1940s. Drug-resistant TB is becoming a global threat due to overuse of antibiotics.

ethnography The systematic social-cultural study of people, often referring to the written account of such research.

genome All the genetic material of an individual organism.

identity politics Similar to the concept of allegorical attraction (where people of similar backgrounds are attracted) identity politics describes the formation of political networks based not on political party but instead on shared family, religion or social background.

indigenous A term used to describe the earliest inhabitants of a region and their living descendants.

medical anthropology Branch of anthropology concerned with the factors that influence human health, the experience of being ill and treatment and prevention of disease.

mitochondria Organelles found in animal cells that act like a battery for the cell. They break down nutrients to generate energy for the cell's biochemical processes.

nationalism The identification of people with a country based on shared ideals and objectives. During the nineteenth century in Europe it was a key driving force behind state formation and imperial expansion.

nuclear transfer A cloning technique that removes the DNA from an unfertilized egg and replaces it with the DNA of the organism to be cloned (contained in the nucleus). The most famous example of nuclear transfer is Dolly the sheep.

ozone layer A gas-based shield found in the Earth's stratosphere. It is made up predominantly of ozone and acts as a giant sponge soaking up large amounts of ultraviolet radiation from the sun.

relativism A method used in social anthropology whereby the researcher attempts to suspend their own cultural ideas and biases in order to understand local beliefs and practices within the context of where they are found.

social anthropology Branch of anthropology that studies human societies and culture.

structural violence Process whereby an institution or social structure causes harm to people by impinging on their basic needs, for example, by institutional racism or sexism.

superficial vein patterns A technique used in forensic identification. Photographs of a person can be used to match the patterns of veins in the skin of a body much like a fingerprint can be matched to its owner.

Terminator A 1984 film in which an intelligent cyborg is sent back in time by a sentient computer to prevent the humans winning a future war against the machines.

transnationalism The phenomenon of ever increasing links between people across the globe that has, to an extent, diminished the importance of national boundaries. In the twenty-first century the growing use of social media has increased the perception of transnationalism as a growing movement.

universalism A dual-concept in social anthropology arguing that all human groups are inherently equal and that many forms of human behaviour and social structure can be observed in all human societies.

ETHNICITY

the 30-second anthropology

Ethnicity is socially constructed.
Human beings develop an ethnicity flexibly on the basis of characteristics they presume they have in common and which distinguish them from other people. These might include gender, language, culture, religion, skin colour, kinship or nationality. This is the view of modern anthropology. What's more, a sense of ethnicity may change greatly over time – as Norwegian anthropologist Fredrik Barth argued. Just when and how a particular ethnicity emerges can be very difficult to analyse. It may be imposed by a state or a bureaucracy or emerge through members of a social movement reacting to a perceived imposition. British-Czech social anthropologist Ernest Gellner, for example, proposed that far from being old, nationalist movements are inherently modern – and emerge when people feel that they are being excluded from the social mobility associated with industrialization. Contrariwise, nation-states often attempt to encourage a sense of uniformity, promoting a particular ethnicity at the expense of any other that might otherwise emerge. The resulting dynamic situation is rendered even more unstable by globalization, which facilitates the movement of people across national boundaries, who may regard themselves as possessing multiple ethnic identities.

RELATED TOPICS
See also
GENDER
page 128

GLOBALIZATION
page 148

3-SECOND ORIGIN
Ethnicity refers to the different and multiple ways in which a person can identify with a wider group.

3-MINUTE DESCENT
We all use labels to create groupings into which we divide our world. Historically humans used the term 'race' to draw lines between different human groups, often for political reasons. Problematically, 'race' has a strict scientific meaning that has often been lost when it is applied to socially constructed human groups. There are no different human races – just one species. But we are wonderfully varied in terms of our social and cultural structures.

3-SECOND BIOGRAPHIES
MICHAEL BANTON
1925–
British sociologist and anthropologist, a specialist on race and ethnic relations

ERNEST GELLNER
1925–95
British-Czech social anthropologist and philosopher, a pioneer of theories of nationalism

FREDRIK BARTH
1928–2016
Norwegian social anthropologist, whose work explored how groups form boundaries between each other that create ethnic identities

30-SECOND TEXT
David Shankland

Ethnic differences are groups and patterns, such as language, that we can observe in humans today.

WAR & AGGRESSION

the 30-second anthropology

Why do we go to war? A key ingredient of war is aggression and, biologically speaking, this trait is advantageous. It enables animals to fight in defence of resources such as food or to secure mating opportunities. This leads to selection for healthier and stronger individuals who survive and reproduce. Unsurprisingly then, aggression in animals, including humans, is heightened at times of high population densities and resource shortages. Perhaps humans are only different from animals in degree not kind. The combination of big brains, tools and technology allows us to wreak havoc at a far greater scale than other mammals. There is little consensus on how recent large-scale warfare is: it possibly goes back tens or hundreds of thousands of years – it is impossible to know. In reality we live much more at peace than war – the cost of war is too high; it is just that we tend to emphasize war. Working in a period with a recent backdrop of war, archaeologists in Botswana in the 1920s mistakenly interpreted bone tools as weapons; later testing showed they were used for digging termite holes. Popular media also emphasizes stories of 'man the hunter' or 'killer apes' even while humans are mostly cooperative. War could even be interpreted as a form of highly organized, cooperative aggression.

RELATED TOPICS
See also
RITUAL & CEREMONY
page 86

BORDERS
page 104

HIERARCHY & LEADERSHIP
page 122

3-SECOND ORIGIN
Aggression, a feeling of anger or an urge to commit an act of violence, moves in its extreme from individuals to large-scale (armed) conflict between societies: war.

3-MINUTE DESCENT
Bonobos and chimpanzees share 99 per cent of their genome. A river (the Congo) and 2 million years of evolution separate them. In times of conflict chimpanzees are capable of lethal aggression, bonobos resort to sex to restore calm. Chimpanzees live in male-dominated societies, they hunt, use tools and kill. Bonobos' female-led societies show none of these behaviours. Why? Bonobos inhabit more predictable environments, which may allow them to live in more egalitarian, cooperative societies.

3-SECOND BIOGRAPHIES
ASHLEY MONTAGUE
1905–99
British-American anthropologist who worked extensively on race, gender, human aggression and war

FRANS DE WAAL
1948–
Dutch primatologist and ethologist best known for his book *Chimpanzee Politics*, which described the rivalries, conflicts and coalitions seen in chimpanzee groups

30-SECOND TEXT
Djuke Veldhuis

Human aggression has shaped our history as a species.

ARTIFICIAL INTELLIGENCE

the 30-second anthropology

3-SECOND ORIGIN
Artificial intelligence is a branch of science that broadly makes computers do things that require intelligence when done by humans, including learning, reasoning, problem-solving and language understanding.

3-MINUTE DESCENT
In 2011 a computer called Watson, envisioned in 2005 and built by IBM, competed on the US TV quiz show *Jeopardy!* against the show's two biggest champions – and won. Watson ushered in a new generation of technology that could find answers to unstructured data and be effective in understanding and interacting in natural language. Watson has since been used to analyze medical data and identify disease.

We often think of artificial intelligence (AI) as a dream of the future – in the form of science fiction robots with human-like characteristics such as *The Terminator* or *Star Wars*' C-3PO. In reality, AI is already here: your bank, car, home and smartphone all use AI on a daily basis; online virtual personal assistants (such as Siri, Google Now or Amazon's Alexa), that email or phone call from your bank asking about a specific purchase on your credit card, or that song or movie recommendation on your media apps – all are forms of AI. Any program can be considered AI if it does something that would be thought of as 'intelligent' in humans. Today's AI is known as 'narrow' (or weak) AI: it is designed to perform a narrow, specific task – for example, IBM's Deep Blue chess computer, a self-driving car or autonomous weapon. Narrow AI may behave like a human, but tells us nothing about how humans think. For many researchers, the long-term goal is to build 'general' (or strong) AI. This would outperform humans at nearly every cognitive task and also be 'intelligent', meaning that theoretically it could reprogram and improve itself. AI may represent a milestone in human evolution capable of transforming our lives in much the same way stone tools or the discovery of electricity did.

RELATED TOPICS
See also
BRAIN DEVELOPMENT
page 16

GENETIC ENGINEERING
page 142

3-SECOND BIOGRAPHIES
ALAN TURING
1912–54
English computer scientist and mathematician, considered one of the founders of computer science and artificial intelligence

JOHN McCARTHY
1927–2011
American computer and cognitive scientist who coined the term 'artificial intelligence' and was influential in the development of computer programming languages

30-SECOND TEXT
Djuke Veldhuis

Artificial intelligence is the most profound technological change facing humans in the twenty-first century.

ETHICS

the 30-second anthropology

If you compared human groups' differing ethical attitudes to matters such as suicide, marriage, celibacy, adultery, slavery, homosexuality, cannibalism, homicide and human sacrifice, you might decide that there is no one cross-cultural ethical system. Edward Westermarck, one of the founders of the anthropology of ethics in the twentieth century, relied on trying to appreciate human interaction from a local point of view, suggesting that ethical judgements are rooted in locally specific emotional responses. This kind of approach, known as 'relativism', is central to anthropology. To understand and research human behaviours and cultural positions, anthropologists have to suspend any inclination they have towards judgement or disbelief. A classic example is Edward Evans-Pritchard's research on witchcraft amongst the Azande of the Sudan. The question he asked was, 'Why do witchcraft beliefs seem sensible to the Azande?' The answer he gave was that to believe is congruent with their societal norms: that is, they believe that bad things are triggered by anger and resentment, which becomes expressed as witchcraft even if a person is unaware of this process. In turn, the Azande may search for, and accuse, those whom their oracles are said to have revealed as witches.

3-SECOND ORIGIN
An ethical action is something that is morally appropriate, but moral codes differ across the world's cultures – so can we say which one is correct?

3-MINUTE DESCENT
Relativism helps us refrain from judging actions that might seem unusual or unethical from the outside. But it is difficult to reconcile relativism with universalism (the idea that all humans do some things the same way or believe the same ideas), whether in terms of modern scientific knowledge or working towards a global human rights agreement. Inevitably, there is a resulting intellectual tension – anthropologists are forced to be relativists in some contexts and universalists in others.

RELATED TOPIC
See also
FRANZ BOAS
page 60

3-SECOND BIOGRAPHY
EDWARD WESTERMARCK
1862–1939
Finnish ethnographer of North Africa, Bronislaw Malinowski's first teacher, first chair of anthropology at the London School of Economics

30-SECOND TEXT
David Shankland

Ethics are the morals on which we base human rights, although they vary across different groups and cultures.

GENETIC ENGINEERING

the 30-second anthropology

3-SECOND ORIGIN
Genetic engineering offers the opportunity to treat incurable diseases, but may also lead to humanity permanently altering its genetic inheritance.

3-MINUTE DESCENT
The idea of human-made, permanent changes to human DNA presents an ethical dilemma for some people. But not all cultures find the idea of having three (or more) parents confusing for ideas of kinship, or an ethical dilemma. Many cultures have their own systems of inheritance, identity and belonging that place an emphasis on created kinship or the ceremonial formation of a family unit.

Genetic engineering and gene editing can change a person's DNA during his or her lifetime or make permanent changes that will be passed on to descendants. Technological breakthroughs make this possible. Gene editing uses 'molecular scissors' (bacterial enzymes) to cut DNA very precisely: harmful genes are cut out and healthy versions inserted in the gap. Nuclear transfer takes the genetic material of a fertilized egg or adult cell (the nucleus) and transfers it into an unfertilized egg that has had its nucleus destroyed. This is how Dolly the sheep was cloned. Gene editing can treat diseases caused by a mistake in a single gene – for example, fixing the faulty gene (*CFTR*) that causes cystic fibrosis and restoring lung and gut function in sufferers. However, individuals and their families would still be able to pass the faulty, unaltered gene on to their descendants. Nuclear transfer can permanently prevent some genetic diseases. A woman with diseased mitochondria has the nucleus of her fertilized egg added to the empty egg of a healthy woman. This child effectively has three parents: 99.9 per cent of its DNA will come from the mother and father; but 0.1 per cent of its DNA, found in the mitochondria, will come from the female donor. If the child is female, she will pass this genetic change on to her children.

RELATED TOPICS
See also
IDENTITY
page 116

KINSHIP
page 124

3-SECOND BIOGRAPHY
SIR IAN WILMUT
1944–
British embryologist who led the 1996 work to clone the first mammal from an adult cell: Dolly the sheep

30-SECOND TEXT
Charlotte Houldcroft

Humans have been genetic engineers for tens of thousands of years. The creation of clone sheep Dolly is a technical extension from the selective breeding of dogs from wolves in the Ice Age.

26 October 1959
Born in North Adams, Massachusetts, the second of six children

1982
Graduates Duke University in Durham, North Carolina, with a BA in Anthropology

1985
With colleagues, opens a small clinic, Clinique Bon Saveur, in Cange, an impoverished area of Haiti

1987
Establishes Partners in Health (PIH) with Ophelia Dahl, Todd McCormack and, later, Jim Yong Kim

1990
Receives his MD from Harvard Medical School and his PhD from Harvard University. Begins residency at Brigham and Women's Hospital, Boston

1993
Receives MacArthur Foundation 'Genius' Award at the age of 34. He donates this money to PIH

2004
His book *Pathologies of Power: Health, Human Rights, and the New War on the Poor* links structural violence and inequality to suffering, illness and death

2009
Selected as United Nations Special Envoy to Haiti

2010
A 7.0 magnitude earthquake shakes Port-au-Prince. The PIH Zanmi Lasante public health system of clinics and hospitals remains mostly intact and provides immediate aid

2014
Ebola outbreak in West Africa. PIH-supported sites provide 336 beds for emergency healthcare, and also work with the community; they remain afterwards to rebuild and improve the weak health system in Sierra Leone

PAUL FARMER

Paul Farmer first went to Haiti when he was 23 years old, studying for a joint degree in medicine and medical anthropology at Harvard Medical School. Over the years, Haiti would become one of the first and most important sites for the work of Partners in Health (PIH), an innovative global charitable organization that Farmer established five years later in 1987 and which came to the world's attention in the aftermath of the 2010 earthquake near Port-au-Prince. What has made Farmer's work at the intersection of anthropology, public health and development so effective and inspiring has been his insistence that health and social justice must go hand in hand, and that means collaborating closely with local people and investing not only in health interventions, but in much broader social change as well.

Farmer seems the perfect person to dream up something like PIH. He spent his childhood sharing a converted schoolbus and later a houseboat with six siblings in different places around the American South. This unconventional upbringing led to a full scholarship to Duke University, where he not only excelled in anthropology, but also became inspired by the writings of German physician and anthropologist Rudolf Virchow, Norwegian sociologist and mathematician Johan Galtung and African American minister and civil rights activist Dr. Rev. Martin Luther King, Jr. – and the role of public health in social justice.

To the young Farmer, providing health assistance to poor Haitians meant not only supplying medicines and training community health workers (*accompagnateurs*), but also dismantling insidious forms of 'structural violence' and inequality. Doing this meant being able to walk in the Haitians' shoes while reflecting on his own ambiguous role as doctor, researcher or friend. This may have been common among anthropologists in the 1990s, but it was refreshing and revolutionary for international medicine.

Farmer won a MacArthur 'Genius' grant in 1993 (at the age of 34) and expanded PIH to work on the Ebola outbreak in West Africa and on drug-resistant TB in Peru, Russia and Boston. He is chair of the Department of Global Health and Social Medicine at Harvard Medical School and served as UN Special Adviser to the Secretary-General on Community-Based Medicine and Lessons from Haiti.

Jason Danely

THE HUMAN AGE
the 30-second anthropology

Human evolution has largely been shaped by local environmental conditions and global climate change, but now the arrow of causality has been reversed. We influence Earth's biodiversity on an unprecedented scale. We have warmed the planet, raised sea levels and acidified oceans. Our impact is unparalleled and global, directly or indirectly affecting all life on Earth. This has led to a proposal for a new geological epoch – the 'Human Age' or Anthropocene. The exact starting date is under debate. All suggestions coincide with times when geologists thousands of years from now will be able to see a signature of human activity in the Earth's rocks. A global signature of human activity is first visible in the sixteenth century when ice cores show a drop in carbon dioxide – caused by the deaths of 50 million indigenous peoples in the Americas triggered by the arrival of the Europeans. In the aftermath millions of hectares of farmland were abandoned, causing plant regrowth and a reduction in global carbon dioxide levels. Another step change occurred in the mid-twentieth century: mass use of fertilizer, rises in meat production, use of fossil fuels and radioactive fallout from atomic bombs will leave lasting signals in the sediment.

3-SECOND BIOGRAPHIES
RACHEL LOUISE CARSON
1907–64
American marine biologist
and conservationist credited
with advancing the global
environmental movement by
highlighting the damaging
effects of pesticides

PAUL JOZEF CRUTZEN
1933–
Dutch atmospheric chemist and
climate change researcher who
won the 1995 Nobel Prize in
chemistry for his work on the
hole in the ozone layer

30-SECOND TEXT
Djuke Veldhuis

*In 200,000 years
humans have changed
Earth's environment
and altered the fate of
thousands of species.*

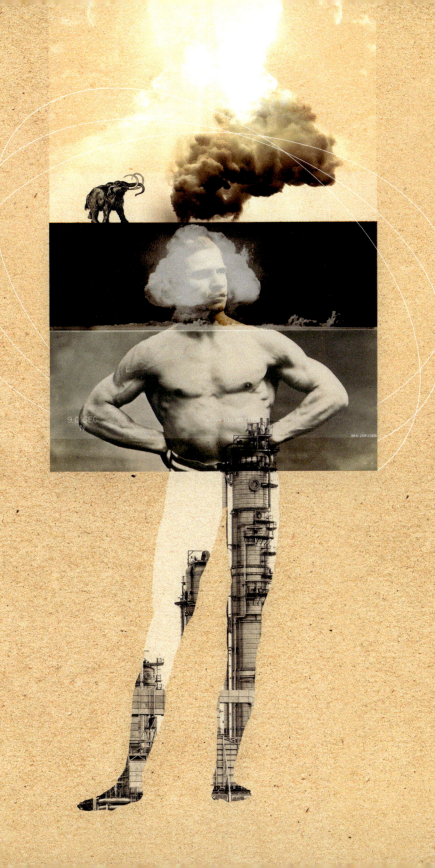

GLOBALIZATION

the 30-second anthropology

3-SECOND ORIGIN
Globalization refers to the process by which the world appears to be getting smaller, linked by a complex web of quickening social and technological interaction.

3-MINUTE DESCENT
Anthropological methods have changed in the face of globalization. Frequently, anthropologists work in more than one field site, leading to 'multi-sited ethnography' and research in any social milieu, whether close to home or abroad. Dominant anthropological theory has changed: before anthropologists might have looked at social organization and kinship, but now identity politics, inequality and transnationalism are becoming popular.

Globalization is conventionally thought to have occurred some time over the last 30 years. But the world's communities have always been to some extent linked with each other. Perhaps what is new is the pace of change, and the increasing complexity with which we are all now connected. Anthropologists are increasingly studying the way that the world's different cultures come into contact with one another; striking phenomena related to globalization include migration and tourism, global economic and capital flows and ritual and cultural transfer across nations or regions. Anthropologists have found the term *glocalization* (a combination of globalization and localization) to be a very useful summary of the way globalization appears to have contradictory effects. It increases homogeneity: an instantly recognizable bland culture of 'consumerized development' with a tendency towards a single language appears ever more dominant. At the same time, it provides unprecedented possibilities for local-interest groups – whether based on religious belief, language, cultural, professional or leisure pursuits – to come together, enabled by the ease of communication and mutual recognition that globalization affords.

RELATED TOPICS
See also
KINSHIP
page 124

ETHNICITY
page 134

THE HUMAN AGE
page 146

3-SECOND BIOGRAPHY
THEODORE LEVITT
1925–2006
American economist and editor of the *Harvard Business Review* who is widely credited with defining our modern understanding of globalization as an economic concept

30-SECOND TEXT
David Shankland

Globalization suggests that, economically and culturally, people across the world have more shared experiences than ever before.

FORENSIC ANTHROPOLOGY

the 30-second anthropology

3-SECOND ORIGIN
Forensic anthropology
is the identification of the
human, or what remains
of the human, for
medicolegal purposes.

3-MINUTE DESCENT
Anatomically trained
forensic anthropologists
can also assist in the
identification of the
living – often from
photographs. This is
most commonly performed
in the investigation of
indecent images of
children. In cases where
a perpetrator is recorded
on an electronic device,
anatomical comparisons
may be undertaken that
will seek to match or
exclude a suspect from
being the possible
perpetrator of the crime.
Features may include
scars, freckles, birthmarks,
superficial vein patterns
and so on.

Forensic anthropology is a
science of identification and usually – though
not exclusively – provides information about
the deceased for criminal investigations. It is
challenging for any police investigation if the
identity of the deceased is unknown. Establishing
the sex, age at death, stature and ancestral
origin of remains will help the police to discover
who the person was in life, while further analysis
may help confirm the manner and cause of
death. It is more difficult to achieve positive
identification if the remains are skeletonized,
scavenged by animals, burned, fragmented or
dismembered and further challenges occur in
cases of mass fatality where remains may have
been disrupted significantly. For example,
following the Asian Tsunami of 2004 more than
one-quarter of a million people died and forensic
anthropology played a large role in returning
identity to the deceased and, in turn, returning
the deceased to their families. Interpol recognizes
three primary sources of identification – DNA,
fingerprints and dentition – but the real
challenge occurs when, for whatever reason,
these methodologies cannot be used. Forensic
anthropology then comes into its own with an
often painstaking restoration of the temporarily
mislaid or concealed identity of the victim.

RELATED TOPIC
See also
IDENTITY
page 116

3-SECOND BIOGRAPHIES
T. DALE STEWART
1901–97
American anthropologist,
founding father of forensic
anthropology and a major
contributor to most areas
of skeletal biology

RICHARD NEAVE
1936–
British facial reconstruction
expert who pioneered the
art and science of facial
reconstruction from the skull

30-SECOND TEXT
Sue Black

*Forensic anthropologists
can use the skull of a
deceased person to
reconstruct a vivid
image of the living
person to help find
their identity.*

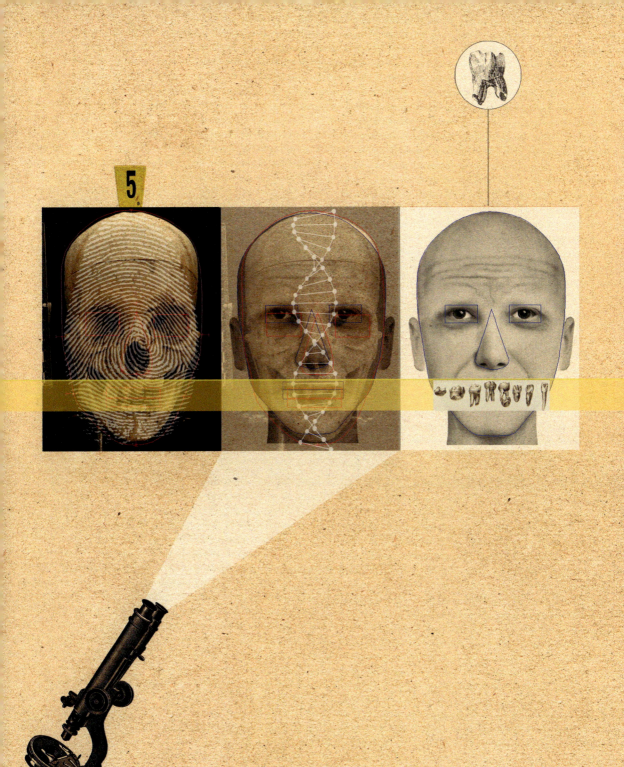

APPENDICES

RESOURCES

BOOKS

50 Great Myths of Human Evolution:
Understanding Misconceptions about
Our Origins
John H. Relethford
(Wiley-Blackwell, 2017)

Anthropology: A Beginner's Guide
Joy Hendry & Simon Underdown
(Oneworld, 2013)

Anthropology: The Basics
Peter Metcalf
(Routledge, 2005)

The Artful Species: Aesthetics,
Art and Evolution
Stephen Davies
(OUP, 2015)

The Artificial Ape: How Technology
Changed the Course of Human Evolution
Timothy Taylor
(Palgrave Macmillan, 2010)

Catching Fire: How Cooking Made Us Human
Richard Wrangham
(Profile, 2010)

Chimpanzee Politics: Power and
Sex among Apes
Franz de Waal
(John Hopkins University Press, 2007)

Human Evolution and Ancient DNA
Simon Underdown & Charlotte Houldcroft
(Routledge, 2018)

The Improbable Primate: How Water
Shaped Human Evolution
Clive Finlayson
(Oxford University Press, 2016)

The Innocent Anthropologist: Notes
from a Mud Hut
Nigel Barley
(Eland, 2011)

An Introduction to Social Anthropology:
Sharing Our Worlds
Joy Hendry
(Palgrave, 2016)

Introductory Readings in Anthropology
Hillary Callan, Brian Street & Simon Underdown
(Berghahn Books, 2013)

Living in a Dangerous Climate:
Climate Change and Human Evolution
Renee Hetherington
(Cambridge University Press, 2012)

Missing Links: In Search of Human Origins
John Reader
(OUP, 2011)

*Neanderthal Man: In Search
of Lost Genomes*
Svante Pääbo
(Basic Books, 2015)

*Social and Cultural Anthropology:
A Very Short Introduction*
John Monahan
(Oxford University Press, 2000)

*The Story of the Human Body:
Evolution, Health and Disease*
Daniel Lieberman
(Penguin, 2014)

*The Tale of the Axe: How the Neolithic
Revolution Transformed Britain*
David Miles
(Thames and Hudson, 2016)

*What is Anthropology? Anthropology,
Culture and Society*
Thomas Hylland Eriksen
(Pluto Press, 2005)

WEBSITES

The Royal Anthropological Institute
https://www.therai.org.uk/

The Leakey Foundation
https://leakeyfoundation.org/

Sapiens – Everything Human
http://www.sapiens.org/

The Pitt Rivers Museum
https://www.prm.ox.ac.uk/

Prehistory of Lascaux-Dordogne – home to
some of the most remarkable prehistoric cave
art in the world
http://www.lascaux-dordogne.com/en/
prehistory

The Neanderthal Museum
https://www.neanderthal.de/en/home.html

The British Museum
http://www.britishmuseum.org/

NOTES ON CONTRIBUTORS

EDITOR

Simon Underdown is Senior Lecturer in Biological Anthropology at Oxford Brookes University. A former Vice President of the Royal Anthropological Institute, he is currently Chair of the Society for the Study of Human Biology and a Research Associate of the School of Anthropology and Museum Ethnography at the University of Oxford. He has written for the *Guardian* on contemporary science issues and appears regularly on TV and radio discussing human evolution and anthropology.

CONTRIBUTORS

Russell Adams is an anthropological archaeologist with primary research interests in the emergence of complex societies and early states and the adoption and development of industrial processes and technology during prehistory. He has been a SSHRC post-doctoral fellow at McMaster University, Ontario and has taught at universities in the UK, Canada and the United States.

Sue Black is Director of both the Centre for Anatomy and Human Identification and the Leverhulme Research Centre for Forensic Science at the University of Dundee. She is a human anatomist and a certified forensic anthropologist with many years of experience working within the UK and internationally. Professor Black received a Damehood in 2016.

Brad K. Blitz is Professor of International Politics at Middlesex University, Visiting Professor at the Institute of Global Affairs, London School of Economics and Senior Fellow at the Global Migration Centre of the Graduate Institute Geneva. He is the author of *Migration and Freedom: Mobility, Citizenship and Exclusion* (Edward Elgar Publishing, 2016).

Jason Danely is Senior Lecturer in Anthropology at Oxford Brookes University. He conducts ethnographic research on ritual and care in the context of Japan's aging society and is the author of *Aging and Loss: Mourning and Maturity in Contemporary Japan* (Rutgers, 2014).

Ken Dark studied archaeology at the universities of York and Cambridge, and has taught at the universities of Oxford, Cambridge and Reading. He has written many books and academic articles, and has directed and co-directed excavations and archaeological survey projects in Britain and the Middle East. He is a Fellow of the Society of Antiquaries of London, the Royal Historical Society and the Royal Institute of Anthropology.

Jan Freedman is the curator of natural history at Plymouth City Museum and Art Gallery. His main interest is in the recent animals from the Ice Age and how humans interacted with them. He is co-founder of and a contributor to Twilight Beasts, a blog which looks at the magnificent creatures from the Ice Age.

Charlotte Houldcroft studied Human Sciences at Oxford University and has a PhD in molecular biology from Cambridge University. She has a special interest in the infectious diseases that afflicted Neanderthals and our earliest human ancestors.

Marta Mirazón Lahr is a Reader in Human Evolutionary Biology and Director of the Duckworth Laboratory, Department of Archaeology and Anthropology at the University of Cambridge. Her research interests cover many aspects of human evolution and she is the author of *The Evolution of Modern Human Diversity* (Cambridge University Press, 1996).

Michael Bang Petersen is a professor in political science at Aarhus University in Denmark. He has done extensive research on the evolved underpinnings of modern political behaviour.

Joshua Pollard is a Reader in Archaeology at the University of Southampton. His interests relate to material culture, landscape, early monumentality and the later prehistory of northwest Europe. In recent years he has conducted archaeological excavations in the Stonehenge and Avebury World Heritage Site.

David Shankland is Director of the Royal Anthropological Institute, and Honorary Professor in Anthropology, University College London. He studied initially at Edinburgh, and then at Cambridge, where he conducted his PhD fieldwork in Turkey, examining questions of rural social change, politics and religion, then worked as Assistant Director of the British Institute of Archaeology at Ankara, before taking up lectureships, at the University of Wales Lampeter, and then Bristol University.

Djuke Veldhuis is a research fellow at the Aarhus Institute of Advanced Studies (AIAS) at Aarhus University in Denmark. She studied at the University of Cambridge and has diverse research interests centred on human behaviour, health and anthropology.

INDEX

ACKNOWLEDGEMENTS

Simon Underdown would like to thank Jemma Underdown for her enormous help and Joanna Bentley for her advice and support.

The publisher would like to thank the following for their permission to reproduce the images in this book.

Alamy/Avalon/World Pictures: 59LC; Zuma Press Inc: 144L. Brooklyn Museum: 51CR, 51BL, 91TL. Clipart.com: 15R, 17L, 67R, 75L, 75TR, 75BL, 75B, 93C, 143T & C, 147L, 151BL. Getty Images/Bettmann: 6oL; GraphicaArtis: 69L; Print Collector: 129T; Ulf Andersen: 120C. Randall Hagadorn, Institute for Advanced Study: 102L. Library of Congress, Washington DC: 8L, 49C, 69TL, 69TR, 77B, 87C, 107C, 115TL & TR. London School of Economics: 78L. Los Angeles County Museum of Art, www.lacma.org: 63C, 63CR, 63CL, 67LC. Metropolitan Museum of Art: 59BL, 59BC, 59BR, 63CR, 63TC. Nationaal Archief/Anefo/ Rob Bogaerts: 26L. National Gallery of Art, Washington: 89C. New York Public Library: 37C. Rijksmuseum: 101C. Science Photo Library/Matteis/Look at Sciences: 151C. Shutterstock/1989studio: 49C; Adriana Iacob: 91L; Alberto Loyo: 45C; Alexandra Giese: 45C; AlexAranda: 67B; Alexey Boldin: 139CR; Andrey Burmakin: 117B; Anna Hoychuk: 87T; Anna Jurkovska: 101BL; Anton Ivanov: 105CL; Anton Watman: 141BC; ArCaLu: 45C; BEGUN: 105C; Beker: 29C; bekulnis: 19C; benkworks: 143BG; binik: 83; BMJ: 105TR; boreala: 49B; Brandon Alms:; 151TL; BrAt82: 123BL; Buslik: 21TC; bymandesigns: cover; carlos castilla: 125LC; Chantal de Bruijne: 45BG; chippix: 35T, 75TL, 123UC; Chones: 149B; Cienpies Design: 135; corund: 89C (BG); Cranach: 139B; DarkBird: 83BL; demidoff: 45R; Dizain: 135; Dominique Landau: 53BG; donatas1205: 51C; Donna Beeler: 123B; Dream Master: 35M; Dutourdumonde Photography: 21CB; dvande: 67UC; DW labs Incorporated: 17C; eladora: 81L&R; Elenamiv: 125BG; Elina Li: 115BG; Elzbieta Sekowska: 77TL, 147C; Enrique Alaez Perez: 49LC, 91TL; Ev Thomas: 67TL; Everett - Art: 115C; Everett Collection: 21C, 119C; Everett Historical: 43C, 43BR, 85B, 105B, 107BR & BL, 137T, 137B, 147T; Evgeniia Ozerkina: 119UC; Evgeniya Fashayan: 139C; FenlioQ: 47CR; Finchen: 139BL; Fishman 64: 19B; Focus no.5: 91R; Fokin Oleg: 63BC; frescomovie: 125; frikota: 51C; Funky BDG: 123M; Gallinago_media: 105TL; Gencho Petkov: 17T; Gerasimov_foto_174: 19R; German Ariel Berra: 117B; GOLFX: 91M; green space: 85T; gualtiero boffi: 117B; Gyuszko-Photo: 49UC; Hein Nouwens: 21BL, 23BL, 83, 89C, 127C, 137CL, 139TL; Iakov Filimonov: 21T; Iestyan: 117C; Igor Zh: 115T (BG); ilolab: 21BG; iryna1: 117C (BG); Ivan Cholakov: 49T; Ivonne Wierink: 67C; Jag_cz: 23T; Jana M: 37C; Johan Swanepoel: 39C; Jolygon: 17L; joppo: 87B; Joshua Haviv: 77C; jps: 23B; JVrublevskaya: 65L; kak2s: 143UC; karbunar: 122C; Kevin L Chesson: 117B; Khomkrit Songsiriwith: 115BG; kkays2: 149TC; Kokoulina: 19L; komkrit Preechachanwate: 15, 125C; Kues: 89BG; Labetskiy Alexandr: 117B; Lienhard.Illustrator: 39C; LiliGraphie: 87R; Liu zishan: 139TR, 149C; Lynea: 17T, 69BR, 89T, 129BR, 129BC; Mad Dog: 151C; maga: 141B; Maisei Raman: 129BR; Maksim Shmelijov: 149TL; MarcelClemens: 109T (BG); Margaret M Stewart: 81L; Marsan: 137C; Marzolino: 37R, 51BG, 69B, 99TL, 119B; Matteo Chinellato: 29TL; Maxim Gaigul: 139BR; Melanie Ruhnke: 53C; melis: 117C (BG); Melissa Madia: 85T; Michael: 101T; Mikhail Pogosov: 37CR; MilousSK: 85C; Monkey Business Images: 149B; Moolkum: 93B; Morphart Creation: 17R, 19TL, 59T, 89C; natixa: 37C; Neale Cousland: 53C; Nerthuz: 137CR; nikiteev_konstantin: 115BG; Nixx Photography: 143R; Okawa Photo: 75UC; oksana2010: 85C; Oleg Golovnev: 117C; Oleg Znamenskiy: 45TL; Oleksandr Molotkovych: 39C; Olga Rom: 115BG; Only background: 115BG; Orlok: 109L; Ortodox: 75UC; Ozerina Anna: 127BG; Pack-Shot: 49C; Patrick Rolands: 119B; Paul Picone: 101BR; photocell: 149BG; photofriday: 149TR; Physicx: 129C; Picsfive: 125; piyaphong: 93T; pockygallery: 17BG; PomInOz: 53B; Potapov Alexander: 21B, 21BR; Pritha Photography: 109T (BG); PsychoShadow: 141BG; ravl: 100BG; Rawpixel.com: 25C, 135; Renata Sedmakova: 7R; Robbi: 15C; Roman Nerud: 123T, 123C; run4it: 15; Sadik Gulec: 109B; SantiPhotoSS: 115C; schankz: 119TR; Sean Pavone: 107C; Seita: 109C; Sergey Kohl: 19BR; Sergey Le: 65B; Sergiy Zavgorodny: 37C; siloto: cover; somersault1824: 39B; steve estvanik: 43C; stockcreations: 29M; stockyimages: 127; Super Prin: 129BR; Suphatthra China: 29BL; Susan Law Cain: 89C; Suwin: 19T, 147B; svetara: 51BG; Tamara Kulikova: 123B; thebigland: 77C; Theeradech Sanin: 15BG; Tim UR: 29BL; toeytoey: 143B; Toluk: 143T (BG); TonTonic: 77TR; trancedrumer: 147T; Triff: 69B; vaalaa: 77LC; Vadim Petrakov: 51BR; Vector Tradition SM: 141T; Vladimir Zhoga: 81C; Vladystock: 139TR; vvoe: 65B; whiteisthecolor: 135; Whitevector: 119C; Will Rodrigues: 81B; williammpark: 151L; wimammoth: 47L; Wolf Avni: 45R; wongwean: 147T; Woodhouse: 81B; xpixel: 29BG, 125BG; YC_Chee: 6L; yurchello108: 35B; Zelenskaya: 65BR; Zoltan Gabor: 83B; ZoranKrstic: 107BG; ZynatiszJay: 139CR. Smithsonian Institution: 40L. Walters Art Museum: 91L, 91TR. Wellcome Library, London: 47C, 47R, 47BG, 89R, 99B, 151TR & CR. Wikimedia Commons/Cicero Moraes: 15T; Claude Truong-Ngoc: 67R; Daderot: 51TC; Geographicus: 99BG; Gesamt: 15L; Guérin Nicolas: 19C; Klaus D. Peter, Wiehl, Germany: 49LC; Rameessos: 49B; Tasman: 99R. Yale University Art Gallery: 101C.

All reasonable efforts have been made to trace copyright holders and to obtain their permission for the use of copyright material. The publisher apologizes for any errors or omissions in the list above and will gratefully incorporate any corrections in future reprints if notified.